WHEN WE TRUST GOD

Embracing the Relationship That Changes Everything

Laura Lopez-Arenas

When We Trust God: Embracing the Relationship That Changes Everything

The events and conversations in this book have been set down to the best of the author's ability. Some names and details have been changed to protect the privacy of the individuals.

Copyright © 2025 Laura Lopez-Arenas

Scripture quotations marked (NLT) are taken from the *Holy Bible*, New Living Translation, copyright ©1996, 2004, 2015 by Tyndale House Foundation. Used by permission of Tyndale House Publishers, Carol Stream, Illinois 60188. All rights reserved.

Scripture quotations marked (NIV) are taken from the Holy Bible, New International Version®, NIV®. Copyright © 1973, 1978, 1984, 2011 by Biblica, Inc.™ Used by permission of Zondervan. All rights reserved worldwide. www.zondervan.com The "NIV" and "New International Version" are trademarks registered in the United States Patent and Trademark Office by Biblica, Inc.™

All rights reserved. No part of this book may be reproduced or used in any manner without written permission of the copyright owner except for the use of quotations in a book review.

ISBN: 979-8-9892686-4-1 (paperback)
ISBN: 979-8-9892686-5-8 (e-book)

Edited by Nancy Albright
Formatted by Daiana M

Dedication

This book is dedicated to my Lord and Savior. Thank you for nudging me to keep writing when I didn't believe in myself. I am grateful for the gifts you have given me that made this book possible. I am your humble servant and will continue to be a witness to your love and mercy.

To the love of my life, Alex. You were so patient when I wrote my first book. You were probably hoping that I would only write one, but surprise, here we go again. Love you to the moon and back. Thank you for being you.

To my sister, Jennifer. Thank you for allowing your little sister to support you in your faith. Our conversations and your experiences have inspired much of the content.

To my friend, Lana. Thank you for always reminding me to write things down. Your reminders gave me a head start writing this book. I love you and cherish our time together.

Note to the reader: I had no idea that I would be here writing another book. I believe it is God's will, and it is only through His glory that I am able to write. A portion of the proceeds from my books will always be donated, and because of your purchase, together we will spread love, hope, and faith wherever it is needed. My dream continues as I pray that you find hope for your future and begin to experience the love God has for you.

Table of Contents

Introduction	1
Chapter 1: I've Been Changed	7
Chapter 2: A Crazy Kind of Love	15
Chapter 3: Struggling With Faith	27
Chapter 4: Understanding Sin	41
Chapter 5: The Freedom in Surrendering to God	53
Chapter 6: Building a Relationship	67
Chapter 7: Do I Have to Attend Church?	81
Chapter 8: Sharing the Good News	91
Chapter 9: Creating a Wedge	99
Chapter 10: The Joyful Giver	107
Chapter 11: Speaking Life	119
Chapter 12: The Power of God	127
Chapter 13: Our Extraordinary God	139
Chapter 14: Our Daily Bread	147
Chapter 15: The "D-Word"	157
Chapter 16: Being Obedient	165
Chapter 17: The Power of Intention	177
Chapter 18: The Power of His Love: Stories of Transformation	189

Introduction

God works in mysterious ways to say the least. I never intended to write a book, yet here I am finishing the second. After much advice and many edits, I realized that my first book, a memoir called *Better Than I Imagined: Transformed by the Love of God*, needed to be solely about my journey to find God and the beautiful life that was possible only through knowing Jesus. While writing that memoir, I continually felt the need to share what I had learned during my transformation. I guess because that is who I am by nature. That is the talent God has given me. For almost twenty years I was an elementary school teacher. It is my passion to help others learn and grow, only now my curriculum and audience are different.

Like many of you, I have my own set of struggles and triumphs. I talk about some of these in my first book, however,

I do not explicitly address the processes, realizations, and tools that helped me through those challenging times. In this book, I offer guidance on overcoming obstacles that prevent us from trusting in God and having a relationship with Him, and addressing how true transformation happens.

One morning, after praying, I was writing in my journal when I received a message from God: you will write another book. Before my first book was published, I began crafting the one you are now reading. I like writing, but never imagined I would be an author. However, I have learned that when God talks to me, I listen and obey. To be quite honest, I don't feel good enough or equipped enough to do what He calls me to do. I often ask myself, "Who am I to give advice?" But friends, that is the wrong question. The better question is "Who is God?" I can write this book only because He gives me the support, wisdom, and courage to do so. His promise gives me confidence as I move forward in faith, and I now understand how Moses felt when God commanded him to speak to a group of people.

> *"Moses said to the Lord, 'Pardon your servant, Lord. I have never been eloquent, neither in the past nor since you have spoken to your servant. I am slow of speech and tongue.' The Lord said to him, 'Who gave human beings their mouths? Who makes them deaf or mute? Who gives them sight or makes them blind? Is it not I, the Lord? Now go; I will help you speak and will teach you what to say.'" (Exodus 4:10–12 NVI)*

When God calls on you to carry out a task, He will make a clear path. Our job is to trust and have faith. We do not have to feel capable, because through God we can do all things. This book is proof of my faith and obedience.

Over the years, I have read many spiritual books and self-help books. As much as I love being a teacher, I also love being a student. For that reason, I have taken certification courses on stress management and building resilience. I am also educating myself on the Bible. I noticed that so many of the books I was reading were written by religious leaders and figures, but felt that people needed to hear about how the average person comes to know Christ. I know this book will give you encouragement and guidance.

I want you to live your best life filled with joy, purpose, love, and peace. I want you to know and trust Jesus. I want you to be able to brush off the stresses of the flesh and focus on God and eternity. You may already be committed to taking care of your mind and body, but you also need to feed your spirit with righteous things of God, so your spirit can lead you rather than allow your mind, emotions, and body to call the shots on earth. Not to mention that your spirit is the only part of you that matters when it comes to eternity. Your spiritual health determines where you spend eternity, not your six-pack. Not to say that a flat stomach is bad, but it shouldn't be more important than spiritual growth.

Maybe this concept of eternity is too far-fetched for you right now. Let's look at it from an everyday, practical perspective. I was in the best shape of my life, had wonderful friends and family and a great job, and practiced self-care and stress management techniques, but I didn't know Jesus and my life felt incomplete and dull. When you are connected to God, the goodness He offers your soul will seep into your mind and body. We need to care for our whole being and not just its parts; we are only as good as each part. We operate like cars: all the parts are connected, and if one part fails, the car can't and won't run efficiently. This doesn't mean since I know God I can sit on the sofa all day and eat potato chips and ice cream. With God, I want to be better in all aspects of my life. I want to take care of the body, soul, and spirit that God gave me.

This book may challenge some of the beliefs you have been passing off as truths. I know this because I address many of the lies I once believed. If you want to know God, you will need to sort through your life, and evaluate what is drawing you closer to Him and what is pulling you away.

We need to be rooted in God first. Like a tree without a stable root system, the tree does not get fed. It would not be able to stand upright. It would not be able to grow. The roots are the foundation of the tree. God is the root system that makes everything possible in your life. God is the glue that holds your life together. Through Him, all things are possible. Your health, wealth, joy, peace, relationships, and job are contingent upon maintaining your focus on Him. Focus on His will, take action, and patiently wait for Him to do what He does best—create opportunities and provide you with blessings.

CHAPTER 1

I've Been Changed

I've been changed. It was not something I did, and I can't really explain how it happened. How could I? I can't begin to understand God's ways and His miraculous power to make the impossible possible. But I do know I'm different now, and that God made that difference. He healed my pain, corrected my failures, and showed me the path to Him. After all my failures and mistakes came crashing down on me, I knew that I needed to make some big change, but didn't know where to begin. Trying to change through my own volition only led to more failure. I had to admit to my weaknesses and need for God's assistance. Admitting our weaknesses is a challenge, but it is when we acknowledge our weaknesses that we make room for God's perfect power. As hard as it is to admit, admitting our weaknesses is the first step. For example, most of my life I have been a very impatient person. I didn't want to be, but often found myself hurting the ones I love the most, which hurt me as well. I made many sincere attempts to do better, but always fell short. I have come to believe that we are not capable of change without God. It is only through Him that I have become more patient.

Our weaknesses give us the opportunity to witness the depths of His love and mercy—without our failures we would not need God's grace. Acceptance of our weaknesses is admitting to God that we can't do this on our own, that we need Him to renew us. Accepting our weaknesses opens our hearts and allows us to surrender to God. God can meet you wherever you are, and guide you to where you need to be. It was in my darkest and most hopeless moments that I found God. I remember the day I finally admitted that I was in an emotionally abusive marriage with a man who had a prescription drug problem. I knew I could not fix it alone and reached out to God for help.

Spiritual transformation looks very different than other types of transformation. When we transform our physical appearance through diet and exercise, the transformation is obvious to the people around us; the physical changes in our size and structure are noticeable. Spiritual transformation reminds me of the transformation of a butterfly. The caterpillar's changes are not visible. She goes behind closed doors in silence, where no one can witness how the changes happen. Then one day, out of the cocoon pops a beautiful butterfly. No one recognizes her and now she has wings to fly.

Spiritual transformation happens in a similar fashion. Most of the work we do happens within the silence between you and God. It happens in the quiet moments that we spend with God each day. Change can be found in a whisper from your Heavenly Father or a convicting feeling. It can be found in the tears we cry that only God can see. The way in which God is moving in our hearts and minds is invisible, yet spectacular.

You might question if progress is truly possible, wondering how you can possibly change how you think and feel. Let me assure you that you can't make the change, but God can. Each day, if you are willing to surrender to God, He can and will transform you little by little to the depths of your being. You may appear to be the same person on the outside, but you will start to feel different. Then, one day, someone notices your inward changes because those changes have pushed their way out. They can't quite put their finger on it, but they know you are different. It is in that moment that you look up and praise God for His goodness because He is that difference.

> "Anything is possible if a person believes."(Mark 9:23)

I believe that forgiveness is one of those things we can't do alone. There have been people in my life who have cut me deeply, whom I trusted and cared for. I had the desire to put the past behind me, but often found myself angry and reliving those painful moments. When I finally reached my breaking point, I went to God with my pain and a genuine desire to forgive. Sitting on my bed, crying to God, I admitted that I was holding onto resentment and anger. I wanted to forgive, but I didn't know how and needed His help. As the weeks passed, I noticed feeling lighter. Those painful moments no longer triggered my anger and I felt a sense of peace. That is the type of change God can offer you—change that you never thought possible.

In the chapters to come I will share personal stories, Biblical stories and truths, and tips that have been essential to my transformation. I will also address some misconceptions we might have about God and the church. My hope for you is to open your heart and surrender yourself, so that you may experience a beautiful relationship with God and see all that is possible when you put Him first.

Prayer

Father God, I need you. I want to change, but I don't know how. I am weak and know that only you can provide me with the strength and power to change. I surrender to your will and ask that you help me renew my mind so that I may be changed. I put my life in your hands and believe that you will take care of me. Amen.

Reflect

What is preventing you from believing that change is possible? What beliefs do you have about God that might be hindering your spiritual growth?

Laura Lopez-Arenas

CHAPTER 2

A Crazy Kind of Love

Change is possible for you because you are loved! God offers us this crazy kind of love that you can only experience from Him. Jesus came to earth to share this powerful message of God's unfailing love for mankind. It is because of this love that you can be transformed. The only reason we know how to love is because He first loved us.

> *"We love because he first loved us. He is the ultimate example of love and His holy name is synonymous with love. God is love." (1 John 4:19 NLT)*

> *"Whoever does not love does not know God, because God is love." (1 John 4:8 NIV)*

It is difficult to grasp the depth of God's love because we try to understand through our limited human perspective. We ponder the question, "Why would God love us so much?" Maybe you feel unworthy of His love and wonder how God can love you after all the things you have done. The beautiful news is that God loves you not because you deserve it, but because of who He is: your loving Father and Creator. You can't earn His love, therefore, nothing you do—good or bad—will change His feelings for you. This is probably as difficult to understand as quantum mechanics because it goes against everything you know and have experienced on earth. God is not like anyone you know. The sooner you accept that, the faster you will be able to allow Him to love you truly unconditionally.

Before I truly had a relationship with God, I believed that He loved me more when I followed His rules. Too often religion places more emphasis on following laws than on love. It is no wonder that we can't understand how much God loves us because we don't hear about it enough, or when we do, it is misinterpreted. The Jewish religious leaders in the Old Testament are a good example of becoming more focused on religion than love. They were blinded by Jesus being somewhat of a loving outlaw, not obeying the laws that they held steadfast. This led to their inability to see the truth about who Jesus was and what He came to do. In these next verses, Jesus shows what He values most, loving and caring for His people.

> "Another time Jesus went into the synagogue, and a man with a shriveled hand was there. Some of them were

> *looking for a reason to accuse Jesus, so they watched Him closely to see if he would heal him on the Sabbath. Jesus said to the man with the shriveled hand, 'Stand up in front of everyone.' Then Jesus asked them, 'Which is lawful on the Sabbath: to do good or to do evil, to save life or to kill?' But they remained silent. He looked around at them in anger and, deeply distressed at their stubborn hearts, said to the man, 'Stretch out your hand.' He stretched it out, and his hand was completely restored.'" (Mark 3:1–5 NIV)*

Countless times throughout the Bible, Jesus shows how great His capacity for love truly is. Even after He was beaten and was being nailed to the cross, He showed love and compassion by asking His Father in Heaven to forgive His accusers. In His pain, He was concerned about those causing His suffering.

> "While they were nailing Jesus to the cross, he prayed over and over, 'Father, forgive them, for they don't know what they are doing.'" (Luke 23:34)

This is the character of the God that loves you. There is nothing you can do to separate yourself from His love. I hope this fact gives you confidence and comfort. His death on the cross is the greatest love story ever told. God became man to take on the sins of mankind, so that He could free us of the burden of our sins and make us acceptable to be with Him in eternal life.

> *"God so loved the world that he sent his one and only son, that whoever believes in Him shall not perish but have eternal life." (John 3:16 NIV)*

By dying on the cross, Jesus made a way to free us from our sins. He loves us so much that, although He was sinless, He died on the cross so that our sins may be forgiven. It is by His blood that we are cleansed of our sins. He paid the price so we didn't have to. This act alone calls for His name to be honored and glorified.

Here is the deal: your good deeds can't and won't earn you a place in Heaven. You can volunteer every week, buy food for the poor, help the little old lady at the grocery store with her bags, yet you can still find yourself in hell. In the past, I thought this wasn't fair. I wondered why a "good person" might go to hell. That didn't seem right to me. But in fact, this *is* fair, and more importantly, God-honoring.

There are some who are not capable physically, financially, or mentally to do good deeds. This levels the playing field for everyone. There is one way and one way only to enter into God's Kingdom, and that is through Jesus Christ. If our deeds earned us a spot in Heaven, then we would minimize what Jesus did when He died on the cross for us. We would be taking away His glory. His loving act opened up a spot for you in Heaven. You just need to accept Him as your Savior. More later about how to do that. Let's get back to God's love.

There are many stories in the Bible that illustrate Jesus's love for mankind. Let's take a look at a few more just in case you are not convinced that Jesus loves you.

> *"A man with leprosy came to Him and begged Him on his knees, 'If you are willing, you can make me clean.' Jesus was indignant. He reached out his hand and touched the man. 'I am willing,' he said. 'Be clean!' Immediately the leprosy left him and he was cleansed."*

Jesus looked at this man with love and compassion. He saw the man in this painful affliction and wanted to help. He didn't ask questions; He just wanted to take away the man's suffering. This is how God looks at us. Now, let's look at a story that illustrates how God desires for us to love Him back.

> *"As Jesus and his disciples were on their way, he came to a village where a woman named Martha opened her home to him. She had a sister called Mary, who sat at the Lord's feet listening to what he said. But Martha was distracted by all the preparations that had to be made. She came to him and asked, 'Lord, don't you care that my sister has left me to do the work by myself? Tell her to help me!' 'Martha, Martha,' the Lord answered, 'You are worried and upset about many things, but few things are needed—or indeed only one. Mary has chosen what is better, and it will not be taken away from her.'"* (Luke 10:38–42 NIV)

This is such a profound story. At a quick glance, it appears that Martha is doing the right things: being a good hostess, preparing and caring for her guest. However, Jesus is commending *Mary* for *her* behavior. Mary is focused on her guest in a different way with her time and attention. This shows how Jesus loves our attention and desires our connection. This is the same Jesus we know today—the one who wants our time, attention, and love. We can easily get caught up "doing" for God, which is not wrong, but we must also have a desire to "be" with Him.

It is this deep love that Jesus has for His children that causes Him to want us to have an abundance of love, joy, and peace. His grace flows continuously. You are probably wondering, "What's the catch?" The only thing you need to do is believe that He is who He says He is—your Lord and Savior, the one and only Son of God who died so your sins may be forgiven. It is hard to accept that anyone could love us that much, especially if we have never experienced love and care from our parents or spouses. God can't be compared to anyone on earth because He is not of this earth.

Part of the reason many of us can't accept this truth is because we don't feel worthy of being loved. You may feel too far gone and trapped in the chains of sin that you can't escape. Here is the thing: we are not worthy of His love, none of us are, but that doesn't stop Him from giving it to us freely. The heavens rejoice when we make the decision to follow God. He is overjoyed when his lost children find their way home.

> *"Suppose one of you has a hundred sheep and loses one of them. Doesn't he leave the ninety-nine in the open country and go after the lost sheep until he finds it? And when he finds it, he joyfully puts it on his shoulders and goes home. Then he calls his friends and neighbors*

together and says, 'Rejoice with me; I have found my lost sheep.' I tell you that in the same way there will be more rejoicing in heaven over one sinner who repents than over ninety-nine righteous persons who do not need to repent." (Luke 15:4–7 NIV)

There is nothing you can do that will ever take God's love from you. He might dislike your bad choices and sins, but He is always merciful and loving. God's hand is always stretched out, reaching for you.

"Surely the arm of the LORD is not too short to save, nor his ear too dull to hear. He is patiently waiting for you to make the decision to grab hold of him and never let go." (Isaiah 59:1 NIV)

There is one movie and one television series that I recommend you watch to begin to grasp the kind of love God is offering you. Both were monumental in my transformation. *The Passion of the Christ* by Mel Gibson and *The Chosen* by Dallas Jenkins will change your life. *The Passion of the Christ* is hard to watch because the brutality that Jesus experienced is beyond comprehension. You will be tempted to turn it off, but don't. Instead, think about the emotions you experience as you are watching it and then reflect on the pain Jesus endured for you. At any moment, he had the power and authority to stop the beating, but he didn't. Why? He wanted to show the extent of His perfect love. He endured that pain to make a way to be with you for eternity.

The Chosen is about the life of Jesus and His ministry. This is a profound series that brings the Bible to life. There are parts that will make you cry, but the humor will make you chuckle as you imagine that Jesus might have had a similar sense of humor. This series helped me relate to the Bible. As I watched, I wondered if Jesus's story was being accurately portrayed. During each episode, I found myself pausing and using the Bible to confirm that the scene was historically accurate. This confirmation sparked my excitement about knowing the Bible.

Now that we have established how much God loves us, hopefully it will become easier to understand His first commandment. God's greatest commandment is for you to love Him. What is there not to love about Jesus? He is patient when we make mistakes, protects us from evil, and provides for us in times of need. He forgives us when we make mistakes and wants to bless us. He listens to us when we are in trouble. It is easy to love someone who only wants the very best for us. God also calls us to love others—we must love others—as in *everybody*. Yikes! We are part of God's family and therefore brothers and sisters through Christ.

There is a song by The Beatles called "All You Need is Love." This sounds like a cliché and seems so elementary, but how much greater would the world be if we all loved everyone? Yes, I mean *everyone*. Even the cranky neighbor, the gossipy soccer mom, and the terrorist you see on the news threatening to wreak havoc on the country. This seems impossible, because sometimes we even have trouble loving ourselves and our own family members. It really is an impossible task for humans, but that is where God comes in. He is our perfect role model, and the better you know God the easier it will be to love how He calls you to love. It helps me to remember that God loves everyone despite their flaws. Loving people means seeing past the surface, seeing past their failures and character flaws. It means that we don't have to agree with everyone's decisions and actions, but we do need to pray for them and give them some grace. Remember that it is love that makes the difference, accepting God's love, loving Him back, and then loving others.

Dr. Martin Luther King, Jr. famously stated that, "Darkness cannot drive out darkness; only light can do that. Hate cannot drive out hate; only love can do that."[1] Hate only perpetuates hate, but love has the power to change.

At the end of each chapter in this book there is a prayer, but this particular prayer is very special. Now that you know who God is and how much He loves you, I hope that you are ready to accept Him as your Lord and Savior. If so, say this simple prayer. Have some faith and go for it!

∽

Prayer

God, I need you. I ask that you come into my heart and be my Lord and Savior. I believe that you died for my sins. Please forgive me and help me turn away from sin. I want to make you a priority in my life. Thank you for loving me. Amen.

---
[1] Martin Luther King, Jr., *Strength to Love* (New York: Harper & Row, 1963) 18.

Reflect

What verse or story stood out to you? Do you have a hard time accepting God's love? If so, why?

When We Trust God

CHAPTER 3

Struggling With Faith

Faith is believing in the unseen. Like most people, I have struggled with faith for a variety of reasons. Regardless of what you see as the cause of your faith faltering, the fact remains that we struggle with faith because darkness exists. Evil's sole purpose is to snuff out the light and separate you from God. Anything the devil can do to make you question your faith is a mark in the win column in his book. On an earthly level, there are many reasons we struggle with our faith: loss of a parent that died young, or maybe God did not heal your spouse of a terminal illness. You might not have known God growing up, or maybe you experienced a tragic event that tore your faith apart.

If you have ever watched a loved one suffer from an illness and pass away, then you know the pain is so unbearable at times that you can't fathom how God exists. We toil with questions about how He could allow suffering and pain in our lives. Because we can't seem to locate God in times of need, we turn our backs on Him. The opposite is when pain causes us to run to God. It creates a desire to find the only One who can heal us. When we have exhausted all human options and need some supernatural help, we cry out, "God, if you are really out there, I need you."

> *"He heals the brokenhearted and bandages up their wounds." (Psalms 147:3 NLT)*

It is ironic how pain can drive us toward God or away from Him. For me, my pain has always made me run to God. My issue has always been that I only came to God when I found myself in a dire situation. Once the suffering subsided I would forget about Him until the next incident. That is no longer the case for me. After my last disaster I made a vow to never act that way again, and I have been living in God's presence ever since. I pray that your pain causes you to run to God and that you never stop seeking Him out.

The good news is that even when you turn your back on God he never turns his back on you. He is patient, and eagerly waits for the moment when you reach out to Him. There is nothing He wants more than to rekindle a relationship with you. When we experience suffering, we need God to support and strengthen us so that we can find a purpose for the pain and a way to overcome it. He loves you as you are, even if that means you are angry with Him for a time. Bring your emotions to God and be vulnerable and honest. Seek and you will find Him.

> *"Ask and it will be given to you; see and you will find; knock and the door will be opened to you." (Matthew 7:7 NIV)*

It is important to note that God's character is always the same. He doesn't change just because our circumstances have changed. Your situation might be challenging, but God is always good. Too often, we see God through a tainted lens based on our human condition. Knowing that God is good even when your situation is not should give you comfort and peace.

I love the story of Hannah in the Bible—it is a powerful story that shows faithfulness in all circumstances. Hannah She and another woman named Peninnah were married to a man named Elkanah. Peninnah had children, but Hannah was not able to conceive. Peninnah would taunt Hannah because of this, and Hannah was overwhelmed with sadness and grief. Hannah questioned why the Lord would keep her from having children. Hannah's faith could have waned, but she remained faithful. Eventually, after many years and a promise, God allowed her to bear a son, Samuel, a man who would become a great prophet and appoint a king whose lineage Jesus would come from. Mind-blowing! See *(1 Samuel 1–3)* for the entire story.

"In her deep anguish Hannah prayed to the Lord, weeping bitterly. And she made a vow, saying, 'Lord Almighty, if you will only look on your servant's misery and remember me, and not forget your servant but give her a son, then I will give him to the Lord for all the days of his life, and no razor will ever be used on his head.' As she kept on praying to the Lord, Eli observed her mouth. Hannah was praying in her heart, and her lips were moving but her voice was not heard. Eli thought she was drunk and said to her, 'How long are you going to stay drunk? Put away your wine.' 'Not so, my Lord,' Hannah replied, 'I am a woman who is deeply troubled. I have not been drinking wine or beer; I was pouring out my soul to the Lord. Do not take your servant for a wicked woman; I have been praying here out of my great anguish and grief.' Eli answered, 'Go in peace, and may the God of Israel grant you what you have asked of him.' She said, 'May your servant find favor in your eyes.' Then she went her way and ate something, and her face was no longer downcast. Early the next morning they arose and worshiped before the Lord and then went back to their home at Ramah. Elkanah made love to his wife Hannah, and the Lord remembered her. So in the course of time Hannah became pregnant and gave birth to a son. She named him Samuel, saying, 'Because I asked the Lord for him.'" (1 Samuel 1:10–20 NIV)

Growing up, my sister Jennifer and I had a very similar experience with faith. There was a time that her faith was so strong it could move mountains, and she witnessed the power of prayer at a young age.

I was about eight years old, hanging out with Jennifer on the front steps of our home, bouncing around from step to step. When I became bored I leaped off the top step. Laughter filled the air as I got ready to jump, but the laughter quickly disappeared when my feet landed on the ground and I began to turn pale. The candy I was sucking on had become lodged in my throat. Jennifer quickly raced into the house to find our mother. Mom sprang into action and gave me the Heimlich Maneuver, and the candy popped out of my mouth, bounced, and slid across the kitchen floor. They all breathed sighs of relief, but little did my mom know that the nightmare was only beginning.

That night, I refused to eat. My mom chalked it up to my throat being sore from choking. But the next day and the day after that, I still refused to eat. My parents took me to a doctor who assured them that I was fine and could eat normally, however, I was not convinced. Each day I refused to eat anything solid for fear that it might get stuck in my throat. Weeks and weeks went by, and I was living on ice cream. My family pleaded with me and even tried to bribe me with a trip to Disney World, but I wouldn't budge. My mom cried continuously day after day, worried that I was going to become seriously ill. Concern consumed her and she often resorted to yelling and threatening to take the ice cream away, but my dad always felt bad and gave in.

One night after weeks had passed, Jennifer had a plan and asked if I could sleep in her room. My sister stayed up late praying and writing a letter to God asking Him for help. She placed the letter under my pillow as I slept. The next morning, Jennifer asked if I wanted to eat some eggs with her. I nodded yes as if I had amnesia and didn't recall the events of the past several weeks. The fears that had gripped me disappeared as fast as they had appeared. From that day forward I continued to eat more and more until it was all a distant memory. This memory is confirmation that the Lord hears our prayers and answers them.

> *"I sought the Lord and He answered me, he delivered me from all my fears." (Psalms 34:4 NIV)*

This event filled my sister with confidence in God and she learned that she could trust Him with her problems. However, my sister's faith would be challenged in years to come and she quickly forgot how God had answered her prayers that night. As time passed, when Jennifer's prayers were not answered as she hoped, she blamed God for the things that were going wrong in her life. And just like that, the connection she once had with Him was lost.

Several years after the birth of her first son, Jennifer decided it was time to get pregnant again. She pleaded with God to bless her with another child, but as the months passed and each pregnancy test came back negative, her faith waned, and her frustration and anger grew.

It is easy to lose faith when things don't go our way. It is easy to forget those times when God answered our prayers and kept His promises. We become obstinate and ungrateful. We lose our patience and do not trust in His goodness and faithfulness. God always hears us and answers our prayers even if we don't like His response. Sometimes the answer is yes; sometimes it is no or not yet. Regardless of God's response, we need to know that He never forsakes us or forgets us. He wants the best for us, and sometimes He withholds things to make room for something better. He is waiting for just the right time to answer our prayers, as He did for Hannah, so that His name may be glorified. Having a child seemed hopeless to Hannah, but God had bigger plans.

Faith doesn't mean that you are always happy and get everything you want. Faith is putting your trust and hope in God despite your current circumstances. It is truly believing that you have a Father whom you can trust for love, mercy, peace, strength, and comfort.

God makes many promises in the Bible, but an easy, comfortable life is not one of them. The sooner we accept this truth, the stronger we can allow our faith to grow.

> *"I have told you all this so that you may have peace in me. Here on earth you will have many trials and sorrows. But take heart, because I have overcome the world." (John 16:33 NLT)*

Although God doesn't promise an easy life, there are several promises that He does make. I hope that you find comfort in the verses below and begin to understand that as Christians we can stand firm on these promises.

> *"God is our refuge and strength, and ever-present help in trouble." (Psalms 46:1 NIV)*

"For I am the Lord your God who takes hold of your right hand and says to you, 'Do not fear; I will help you.'" (Isaiah 41:13 NIV)

"Be strong and courageous. Do not be afraid or terrified because of them, for the Lord your God goes with you; he will never leave or forsake you." (Deuteronomy 31:6 NIV)

"The Lord is my Shepherd; I have all that I need. He lets me rest in green meadows; he leads me beside peaceful streams." (Psalms 23:1–2 NLT)

"This I declare about the Lord: He alone is my refuge, my place of safety; he is my God and I trust him." (Psalms 91:2 NLT)

"As the Father has loved me, so have I loved you. Now remain in my love. If you keep my commands, you will remain in my love, just as I have kept my Father's commands and remain in his love. I have told you this so that my joy may be in you and that your joy may be complete." (John 15:9-11 NIV)

"Then Jesus said to his disciples: 'Therefore I tell you, do not worry about your life, what you will eat; or about your body, what you will wear. For life is more than food, and the body more than clothes. Consider the ravens: They do not sow or reap, they have no storeroom or barn, yet God feeds them. And how much more valuable you are than birds! Who of you by worrying can add a single hour to your life? Since you cannot do this very little

thing, why do you worry about the rest? Consider how the wild flowers grow. They do not labor or spin. Yet I tell you, not even Solomon in all his splendor was dressed like one of these. If that is how God clothes the grass of the field, which is here today, and tomorrow is thrown into the fire, how much more will he clothe you—you of little faith!'" (Luke 12:22–28 NIV)

There are two things that have helped me maintain my faith: one is the promises found throughout the Bible, and the second is looking back at my life and identifying all those big and small moments that He has provided for me.

One of my favorite stories in the Bible is the story of Job. I highly recommend reading the entire book of Job, but here are a few chapters to illustrate my point. Job was a faithful servant of God, and he was very blessed because of it. God allowed Satan to test Job because Satan said that the only reason Job was so faithful was because he was abundantly blessed. Evil struck and Job lost everything, including his health. In his affliction, his good friends were not supportive, accusing him of doing wrong, because why else would all this happen to Job? Job was frustrated and angry but never cursed the Lord. He pleaded with Him for mercy, but through it all he remained faithful. I love when God shows His glory and power in *Job Job 38:1–41,* where God explains the depth of His power and teaches us to understand how little we know. We don't have to know everything to have faith. Faith is believing things you can't fully comprehend or see. It is placing your hope in a trustworthy, all-knowing, all-powerful God.

> *"'My thoughts are nothing like your thoughts,' says the Lord. 'And my ways are far beyond anything you could imagine. For just as the heavens are higher than the earth, so my ways are higher than your ways and my thoughts higher than your thoughts.'"(Isaiah 55:8–9 NLT)*

God's ways are always higher than ours, which should give us comfort when we struggle to understand why something is happening. He can give your pain a purpose and use your situation to glorify His name. It helps me put things into perspective and humbles me when I think about how I could possibly question the One who created me and everything around me. Having faith is a choice. Choose to have faith in all circumstances instead of looking for reasons to doubt. Choose to believe in God and put your hope in Him. Surround yourself with faithful people and allow their testimony to grow and strengthen your faith. Praise God when you can see His faithfulness in your life.

∽

Prayer

Lord, I believe in you, but at times I need help with my disbelief. It is easy to trust you when things are going my way, but I struggle to believe your promises when times are difficult. Help me trust in your unfailing goodness and focus on your promises to prosper me and not hurt me. I know that you are with me always. Amen.

Reflect

What causes you to struggle with your faith? Recall an event that helped you with your faith and one that was detrimental.

Laura Lopez-Arenas

CHAPTER 4

Understanding Sin

Sin is essentially giving into the temptation of evil and disobeying God's commands. It is refusing to do what is right and good. Sin is not always a giant-sized event. Sin can also be found in the small moments when we believe a lie, like Adam and Eve believed the serpent's lie. Sin came into existence when Adam and Eve failed to reject the lies of Satan and, because of that, we are all born with a sinful nature. When we sin, we do not honor God. Not all sin might seem big, but all sin leads to a dire consequence—taking you from the will of God. Let's check out Adam and Eve's story to get a good grasp of how this all got started.

"Now the serpent was more crafty than any of the wild animals the Lord God had made. He said to the woman, 'Did God really say, 'You must not eat from any tree in the garden?' The woman said to the serpent, 'We may eat fruit from the trees in the garden, but God did say, 'You must not eat fruit from the tree that is in the middle of the garden, and you must not touch it, or you will die.' 'You will not certainly die,' the serpent said to the woman. 'For God knows that when you eat from it your eyes will be opened, and you will be like God, knowing good and evil.' When the woman saw that the fruit of the tree was good for food and pleasing to the eye, and also desirable for gaining wisdom, she took some and ate it. She also gave some to her husband, who was with her, and he ate it. Then the eyes of both of them were opened, and they realized they were naked; so they sewed fig leaves together and made coverings for themselves. Then the man and his wife heard the sound of the Lord God as he was walking in the garden in the cool of the day, and they hid from the Lord God among the trees of the garden. But the Lord God called to the man, 'Where are you?' He answered, 'I heard you in the garden, and I was afraid because I was naked; so I hid.' And he said, 'Who told you that you were naked? Have you eaten from the tree that I commanded you not to eat from?' The man said, 'The woman you put here with me—she gave me some fruit from the tree, and I ate it.' Then the Lord God said to the woman, 'What is this

> *you have done?' The woman said, 'The serpent deceived me, and I ate.'" (Genesis 3:1–13 NIV)*

God did not command Adam and Eve not to eat from that tree because He was withholding anything from them. He was doing it for their own good. Without sin, they were full of joy, love, and peace. They didn't know evil, shame, anxiety, or guilt. But once they ate the fruit from that tree they became aware of good and evil. Sin pollutes us and destroys our innocence. We believe that we are free to partake in whatever our flesh desires, like watching a scary, demonic movie, gossiping with the neighborhood parents, or watching pornography. Just because we have the freedom to partake in anything doesn't mean we should. It is good practice to look at our actions as either moving us closer to God or further away.

Sin separates us from God and makes us think we are unworthy of His love. That is what happened to Adam and Eve. Once they had the knowledge of evil, they realized they were naked and felt ashamed and hid from God. It's ironic that our sin causes us to move away from God, when in fact, it is just the opposite—because we are sinful, we need God to take away our sins.

> *"For I will forgive their wickedness and will remember their sins no more." (Hebrews 8:12 NIV)*

There is a misconception that Christians don't sin. It's a myth; it's impossible for any human to be sinless. God is the only One void of sin. The good news is that you do not need to be perfect to be a Christian. Christians have accepted Jesus as their Savior and have joined the body of believers trying to be more like Christ. As I have reflected on my life, I have identified reasons why we sin.

- Ignorance: There is a lack of awareness that what we are doing is a sin because we have never read the Bible and simply do not know what God tells us. For example, I used to buy crystals and carry them with me to help with stress and anxiety. I didn't see anything wrong with it and didn't know I was committing the sin of idolatry. Whenever we place something or someone above God or depend on it instead of God, we create an idol and sin unknowingly.
- Selfishness: You are aware that you are sinning but don't care as long as you are personally gaining something. Cheating to get ahead is an example. We all know that it is wrong to cheat, but at times we do it anyway if the benefit is worth it.
- Excuses: I am a good person. It is not a big deal that I _____, God will forgive me. This is one my sister would repeat often. She would say, "God gets me, He knows that I don't mean anything by it when I curse. It is not a big deal." This is taking advantage of God's mercy.
- Hopelessness: I don't have the ability or power to fix myself or my sinful situation. You may think that you are too far gone to return to God. Hopelessness is a pit that is hard to pull yourself out of. We accept the dysfunction in our lives because we don't know God well enough to fully understand that He can see us through.

- Non-believer: There are people who are atheists or agnostics who don't believe in God or the promise of eternal life. They think this life is it.

What category do you fall into? Regardless of where your sin is rooted, the solution is always the same: lean into God. Addressing sin is hard because we must first make our own mistakes. There is a lot of guilt and shame surrounding sin, and often it is too painful and easier to ignore.

> *"Jesus looked at them intently and said, 'Humanly speaking, it is impossible. But not with God. Everything is possible with God.'" (Mark 10:27 NLT)*

God is bigger than your problems with sin. With Him in your corner you can overcome anything. Don't focus on the size of your problem, focus on the greatness of God. In the story of David and Goliath, as David faced Goliath he didn't focus on Goliath's size, strength, and reputation for being a worthy adversary. No! He focused on the greatness of God and the things that God had already helped him to overcome. Focus on God and watch as your problems and sins start to fade.

> *"But David said to Saul, 'Your servant has been keeping his father's sheep. When a lion or a bear came and carried off a sheep from the flock, I went after it, struck it and rescued the sheep from its mouth. When it turned on me, I seized it by its hair, struck it and killed it. Your servant has killed both the lion and the bear; this uncircumcised Philistine will be like one of them, because he*

has defied the armies of the living God. The Lord who rescued me from the paw of the lion and the paw of the bear will rescue me from the hand of this Philistine.' Saul said to David, 'Go, and the Lord be with you.' Then Saul dressed David in his own tunic. He put a coat of armor on him and a bronze helmet on his head. David fastened on his sword over the tunic and tried walking around, because he was not used to them. 'I cannot go in these,' he said to Saul, 'Because I am not used to them.' So he took them off. Then he took his staff in his hand, chose five smooth stones from the stream, put them in the pouch of his shepherd's bag and, with his sling in his hand, approached the Philistine. Meanwhile, the Philistine, with his shield bearer in front of him, kept coming closer to David. He looked David over and saw that he was little more than a boy, glowing with health and handsome, and he despised him. David said to the Philistine, 'You come against me with sword and spear and javelin, but I come against you in the name of the Lord Almighty, the God of the armies of Israel, whom you have defied. This day the Lord will deliver you into my hands, and I'll strike you down and cut off your head. This very day I will give the carcasses of the Philistine army to the birds and the wild animals, and the whole world will know that there is a God in Israel.'" (1 Samuel 17:34–42, 45–46 NVI)

While our sin is not acceptable, we are always accepted by Jesus. Jesus loves the sinner, but dislikes the sin. He is waiting for us to open our hearts so that He can change us. Sin comes in many shapes and sizes and sometimes we are not aware of our sins. Sin is ugly, and harmful to your relationship with God. We live in a world where it is easy to sin. Satan and his minions are patrolling the earth looking for ways to separate us from God. Satan's schemes are to trick us. He nicely wraps sin up in a pretty, Tiffany-blue gift box with a white bow. Satan makes sin look like a well-paved road, only to find out that once you are on it, it is loaded with potholes, cracks, bumps, and detours. Let's take a look at some synonyms for sin, as it can often be difficult to see sin in our lives.

Hate	Impatience	Anger
Jealousy	Rudeness	Judgement
Unforgiveness	Resentment	Greed
Lust	Bitterness	Gluttony
Pride	Selfishness	Idolatry

When we sin, we are not only hurting others, but also ourselves. Let's say you are ready to turn away from your sin. You are probably wondering how you go about doing that.

One decision at a time. It is a slow process, but each time you choose to turn away from sin you are saying goodbye to the old you and welcoming God into your life. You are telling Satan that he can't mess with you anymore and he begins to lose his hold over your life. When you feel like you are slipping back into your sinful ways, it is helpful to rebuke Satan out loud. Give it a try. "Satan, I rebuke you in the name of Jesus Christ."

The truth is, we are not strong enough to combat sin alone. God created us to rely on Him and he wants us to depend on Him. This is where prayer comes in. Pray every day, all day, asking Him to give you the strength to fight sin. You will be amazed at how you begin to notice changes in your words and actions. Maybe you are unaware of the sins you are committing or which areas of your life need improving. Pray! Ask God to show you what you are doing that offends Him. Ask Him to search your heart. One day while praying, I prayed this prayer: "Lord, search my heart and reveal to me what you find offensive." Within a few seconds, God shared an image of me judging someone from the past and then showed me the word "compassion." It was difficult for me to receive that revelation because it was ugly and not who I wanted to be, but I was grateful that I now had an awareness of where I was falling short in God's eyes.

Remember that God's voice is convicting. He shows us what we need to change and helps us find a way. There is hope in conviction. The enemy condemns us for our sins and makes us feel worthless and at fault. The enemy keeps us caught up in sin by making us think that there is no way out. When we feel hopeless, we give up and remain stuck in our sinful behavior. God does not point out your sin to hurt you, but rather to heal you. The bottom line is that sin hurts us and hurts God even more. His objective is to call us into a relationship with Him and free us from the destruction of sin.

∼

Prayer

Lord, I am deeply sorry that I have sinned against you. Please forgive me for _____. I want to do better, but I don't know how. Allow your power to rest on me and give me the strength to overcome evil. Be with me and help me make better choices in the face of darkness. Amen.

Reflect

What are some sins that you find yourself repeating? Are there some sins that you think are not giant-sized events, so they are not a big deal?

Laura Lopez-Arenas

CHAPTER 5

The Freedom in Surrendering to God

For a significant portion of my life I viewed my sins as freedom. God's rules seemed so restrictive, and I looked at God's commands as merely suggestions. Once I became old enough to call my own shots, I tore open the bars of my prison cell and let sin run rampant, only to discover that my sin actually was my prison. All the pain and mistakes trapped my soul and held me back from experiencing the freedom that God offers when we walk with Him.

> *"Not everyone who calls out to me, 'Lord! Lord!' will enter the Kingdom of Heaven. Only those who actually do*

the will of my Father in heaven will enter. On judgment day many will say to me, 'Lord! Lord! We prophesied in your name and cast out demons in your name and performed many miracles in your name.' 'But I will reply, 'I never knew you. Get away from me, you who break God's laws.'" ((Matthew 7:21–23 NLT)

When I first heard these verses I instantly became upset as I imagined being in front of God and having Him uttering those words to me: "I never knew you." Tears streamed down my face as I realized that I had wasted a good portion of my life on things that separated me from God. Despite my profession to be a Christian, I didn't really know Jesus. I was a hypocrite. My life was not rooted in anything Biblical. I falsely believed that I could cherry-pick the Bible's teachings and choose to follow only the commands that suited my lifestyle. Helping the poor was conducive and I enjoyed it, but going to church every Sunday was too laborious for me. It was boring and I didn't see the point.

As we have discussed previously, being a believer means that you have accepted Jesus as your Lord and Savior. Justification is when we are called by God to believe this truth. We become just as if we had never sinned. This can happen after someone knows the entire Bible or it can happen to someone who is just starting to read it. This can be someone who barely attends church or a devoted member of a congregation. One thing is certain: once you accept Jesus as your Savior, you will be transformed and your life will never be the same.

Our faith does not end with just believing in Jesus. Following Jesus means that you will have to start peeling away some layers, shedding those dark parts of you. You won't feel like you "have to," but rather that you "want to." The real work is just beginning: the next step is to become more righteous as you abide in God. This process is called sanctification and is the reason we experience different levels of spiritual maturity. The process of growing as a Christian never ends. I remember feeling disappointed when I accepted Jesus as my Savior. I wondered why I found myself still struggling with sin. Accepting Jesus is not a magic switch that, "poof," makes you perfect, but a step on a path in the right direction.

You can compare this to driving. We can drive once we obtain a license, but it doesn't mean we are good, experienced drivers. As we drive more and encounter different situations our driving improves. Being a Christian works the same way: as we walk with God, read His Word, and pray, we notice a change in our spirituality. The process and time frame are different for everyone. As God works in our lives, we grow and develop into who He is calling us to be.

My freshman year of college, I attended a Catholic University in Connecticut. At that point, I had only been intimate with my high school boyfriend who I was madly in love with. A part of me felt guilty about having premarital relations, but at the same time I felt justified in a sense, like my opinion held more weight than God's Word. This guilt prompted me to go to confession at the school chapel. As I sat face-to-face with the priest, I confessed having premarital sex, but my next words took my arrogance and ignorance to the next level. I said, "Father, but I only had sex with one person I really love. That is so much better than the girls I know who are sleeping around with a new guy every weekend." Ouch! My words were dismissive of the Bible's wisdom, divinity, and power. I cared more about my opinion than what God says. I think so many of us fall into this trap that our "opinion matters." Remember that when your opinion contradicts God's Word, you are wrong.

At that point in my life, I knew of God, but He wasn't my priority. I had the knowledge of God and religion, but had not completely submitted myself to Him. I was testing the water, dipping my toes, but not ready to commit to jumping in feet first. I knew if I jumped in I would become soaking wet; there wouldn't be an ounce of me that was dry. This meant complete surrender to God, and I was not ready for that. I was like a child plugging my ears with my fingers, humming and shaking my head to block out the voice of God. I didn't want to be convicted. I wanted to be "free."

The devil makes sin seem freeing. It is this lie that prevents us from taking the plunge and surrendering to God. If we jump, we must leave everything behind: hate, anger, jealousy, resentment, pain, lust, bitterness, impatience. For a long time, I chose to just get my toes wet because I lacked understanding of how my sin was destroying me. In retrospect, I can see how "living free" led me to destruction. The reality is that God equals peace and sin equals destruction. The devil wants us to believe that God is holding us back just as he convinced Eve.

Once I realized this and gave my life to Christ, the hard work began. So much of my identity was tied up in my sins. It was painful for me to shed who I was and it left me feeling confused and unsettled. In time, I had torn away so many layers that I felt like I had lost my identity—I didn't know who I was anymore. There were the obvious parts of me that I knew had to go, but there were some layers that I didn't think were "too bad." I thought I could hold on to the "minor" sins and inappropriate behavior, but God gently brought those to my attention and said that, yes, those too must go.

For a while, I found myself being a little quieter, feeling like I had nothing to say now that I was no longer me. I could see how it was easier to do the wrong thing rather than the right thing. It was painful to be "good." So many people think that they are tough because they don't take any garbage from people; they are outspoken, get ahead by any means necessary, and live their lives the way they want. Trust me, that is weak! Abiding by God makes you tough.

As I peeled back the layers of who I thought I was, I grew tougher. It was easy to go along with societal norms, to give in to the desires of my flesh and conform with those around me. Life was easy before God because life is easy when you are doing the wrong things. The devil leaves you alone because you are already right where he wants you. When you learn to say no to things that are not of God, life gets challenging. The devil gets flustered because you are changing. He begins to whip out all the tricks from his bag to distract you.

You are probably thinking that you should close this book and continue living how you always have. I have been on both sides and, trust me, living your life with God is better. Growing spiritually is like hiking up Mount Everest. The journey up is painful and challenging, but you keep going because you know the magnificent site that lies at its peak, where the pain of the journey fades and you can bask in the peace and beauty of resting on top of the world. I promise you that following Jesus is worth it.

Growing up Catholic, I always had some sort of faith lingering in the background, but that was where my faith stayed—in the background. I followed God as long as it didn't infringe upon my "freedom." For a while I was a lukewarm Christian, as many people call it. I wasn't a horrible person, but I acted like being a Christian was like Burger King—you can have it your way. Comparing myself to others that were "worse" allowed me to justify my words and actions. It was almost like I thought there was a limited number of seats in hell and if I could just be better than some I would be safe. I figured I could do what I wanted within reason and keep God neatly tucked away until I needed Him. But guess what? Hell has unlimited capacity.

When I decided to dive into the Bible I began to do a lot of self-reflection, which was often very painful. I had to take a good look at the person I had become, and it made me uncomfortable. There were so many areas of my life where I was getting a failing grade. This entire time I had been holding the wrong people up as my exemplar in life. Jesus is the One we need to compare ourselves to and try to emulate. Achieving perfection like Jesus did is impossible because there is only One who is perfect. However, when we wake up each morning we should strive to be more like Jesus and less like ourselves. God knows that we will never achieve this because we were born with a sinful nature. Thank you, Adam and Eve. But that should not prevent us from doing our best. God doesn't deserve any less than our best efforts.

To become your best, you need to start thinking about what you are doing that is separating you from God, and then repent. There seems to be a stigma around sin and repenting. In my mind's eye, I envision a priest yelling from the altar, telling the congregation, "Repent of your sins, you sinners, or be doomed to eternal damnation!" As true as that statement is, repenting simply means turning away from your sin. It means literally turning your back on sin and taking a different path. It doesn't sound so heavy or scary when it is phrased that way. Your sin is holding you back from being the person God intended you to be. It is holding you back from living a beautiful, blessed life and having a close relationship with God. Sin is the wedge that we put between ourselves and God. It is not God's fault, it is ours.

We need to stop making excuses for our actions and start holding ourselves accountable to God's commandants and His will for our lives. We live our lives how we want, not considering what God wants for us, which is his will. We do only what makes us happy and not what makes God happy. He gave us life and our lives do not exist solely for how we want to live them.

This sounds restrictive, but it is quite the opposite. In fact, it is very freeing. You can give up the things in your life that are causing you pain and gain peace, love, and joy instead. Isn't that all we really want anyway?

As I slowly peeled back the layers of who I was, I realized that some layers were easy to shed while others took a little more time. I also noticed that, depending on my environment and the people that surrounded me, it seemed like those layers I had shed somehow grew back. Let me explain.

I started out very simply by giving up cursing. I was ready to permanently remove it from my vocabulary and had been doing a good job until I went back home to New Jersey. My sister's friend picked me up at the airport. He is a super-nice, friendly guy, and as he became more comfortable with our conversation his words became very colorful. All the cursing was like nails on a chalkboard to me; it pierced my soul and sounded so ugly. I was relieved when he dropped me off. My family generally has a very colorful vocabulary as well, and after spending the weekend with them I found myself throwing out a curse word here and there too. The only difference is that now it tasted bad as it came out of my mouth. It was a challenge not to conform to my environment, but I was determined to continue to be the new me.

It can be frustrating and confusing as you let go of the parts of you that you "think" make you who you are. I often wondered who this person was that I was becoming. I remember asking God, "How many parts of the old me do I need to get rid of?" The answer: everything that doesn't reflect Me. I was peeling away the layers to reveal my new identity that was rooted in Jesus. I kept peeling until I started becoming more like Him and less like me. Being more like Jesus means having more patience, being kinder and more generous. It means being helpful and not hurtful. It means being slow to anger and quick to forgive. It means being more loving to everyone. Without trying to emulate Christ, we cannot be Christians.

Even from a distance, there were some people in my life who didn't understand my change. They questioned my transformation and found it somewhat annoying. I know this change was hard on my husband at times. He expressed to me one day that he married me one way and now I was completely different. I didn't argue with him, but prayed instead that he would grow to accept the changes and recognize that they were for the best.

I am more careful now about what I allow to enter my heart. I don't watch certain movies or listen to certain songs anymore because the language robs me of my peace. I avoid gossiping and talking negatively about others. I find myself listening more and speaking less. It is better to be silent than to speak words that God wouldn't approve of. Anything that is offensive to God should offend us as believers.

Some might see me as not as much fun as I once was, but I am alright with that. What I consider entertaining has been redefined. My fun is rooted in goodness, peace, and love. Good or bad, other's opinions of me don't really matter. I became tired of offending God with my actions and words.

I am still a work in progress and far from perfect. Being a Christian doesn't mean being perfect. Each day we should wake up with the intention of focusing on Jesus and being more like Him. Some days will be better than others, but know that God forgives you and move forward. The only real freedom you will experience is found through walking with God. Sin gets in your way of living free, but society would have us believe otherwise. Society says that you are free to be whoever you want, and you can do and say whatever you want.

When I think about everything God has done for me, my heart radiates beams of sunshine and my eyes fill with tears. Jesus suffered a death worse than I can fathom and I cry wondering how I can be loved so much. This is when I realized that letting go of who I was to be who God is calling me to be is a gift, not a sacrifice. God offers each and every one of us freedom by forgiving our sins and offering us a way to change.

Prayer

Lord, please forgive me for my sins. Help me to turn away from the parts of me that are offensive to you. Give me the strength to change and not give into my sinful desires. I want to be more like Jesus. Help me to be in this world, but not driven by worldly desires. Amen.

Reflect

What can you do to improve yourself and start being more like Jesus? How does changing make you feel?

When We Trust God

Laura Lopez-Arenas

CHAPTER 6

Building a Relationship

As Christians, we believe that there is only one God. However, there are three distinct persons that we acknowledge and have a relationship with: the Father, the Son, and the Holy Spirit, who together comprise the Holy Trinity. Humans were made in the image of God and are made up of three parts—body, soul, and spirit—and these parts cannot be separated. However, God can separate the parts of His oneness, and you will notice that all three are referred to in the Bible.

> *"So God created mankind in his own image, in the image of God he created them; male and female he created them." Genesis 1:27 NIV*

Throughout this book I generally refer to God without distinguishing between God, Jesus, and the Holy Spirit. Please know that God the Father is seated in Heaven. God the Son (Jesus Christ) came to earth and became fully man and fully God to die for our sins. God the Holy Spirit was sent to us after Jesus died on the cross to support and guide us.

> "Therefore, go and make disciples of all the nations, baptizing them in the name of the Father and the Son and the Holy Spirit." Matthew 28:19 NLT

Because the only way to the Father is through the Son, building a relationship with Jesus is a vital part of growing your faith. Setting an intention to grow my relationship with Jesus was my starting point for spiritual growth. Like any good relationship, it took time to blossom into what it is today.

Not all relationships are built the same. Many of us have acquaintances that we might see every week at work, but know little about. We may engage in chitchat and know some surface level facts about them, but still never really know them. To know someone means to know their heart. A solid relationship is built on trust, honesty, and love.

The Bible offers a good illustration of a superficial relationship versus a relationship built on a strong foundation. One would think that all the Apostles had a similar relationship to Jesus, but we find that Peter's relationship with Jesus was very different than that of Judas. On the surface, their relationships looked very similar. Both men spent many years with Jesus, listening to Him preach, talking with Him, and watching Him perform miracles, yet one of them did not really know Jesus's heart. Let's take a look at Scripture.

In this verse, Peter, a loyal, faithful friend and servant, makes a grave mistake: protecting himself by denying that he knows Jesus. After doing so he is beside himself, filled with remorse and sadness.

> *"Then seizing him, they led him away and took him into the house of the high priest. Peter followed at a distance. And when some there had kindled a fire in the middle of the courtyard and had sat down together, Peter sat down with them. A servant girl saw him seated there in the firelight. She looked closely at him and said, 'This man was with him.' But he denied it. 'Woman, I don't know him,' he said. A little later someone else saw him and said, 'You also are one of them.' 'Man, I am not!' Peter replied. About an hour later another asserted, 'Certainly this fellow was with him, for he is a Galilean.' Peter replied, "Man, I don't know what you're talking about!' Just as he was speaking, the rooster crowed. The Lord turned and looked straight at Peter. Then Peter remembered the word the Lord had spoken to him: 'Before the rooster crows today, you will disown me three times.' And he went outside and wept bitterly."* (Luke 22:54–62 NIV)

In this next verse, Judas betrays Jesus just as Peter does, however, when he realizes his mistake he commits suicide out of his pain and regret.

> *"Early in the morning, all the chief priests and the elders of the people made their plans how to have Jesus executed. So they bound him, led him away and handed him over to Pilate the governor. When Judas, who had betrayed him, saw that Jesus was condemned, he was seized with remorse and returned the thirty pieces of silver to the chief priests and the elders. 'I have sinned,' he said, 'for I have betrayed innocent blood.' 'What is that to us?' they replied. 'That's your responsibility.' So Judas threw the money into the temple and left. Then he went away and hanged himself." (Matthew 27:1–5 NIV)*

Both men betrayed Jesus, but the outcome for each was very different. One might wonder why. After reading these verses, I wondered why Judas wouldn't confess his sin and ask Jesus for forgiveness—Jesus's entire ministry was about love and forgiveness. But then something occurred to me. Judas didn't truly know Jesus. He didn't understand the love Jesus had for him and was in the relationship for the wrong reasons. He didn't understand Jesus's mission. Peter, on the other hand, had a relationship with Jesus and knew that he would be forgiven. He knew the love Jesus had for him and that mercy was available.

Looking back on my faith I had an epiphany. I can relate to Judas because there is a difference when you "know" someone versus "have a relationship" with them. I "knew" Jesus my entire life, but I never had a "relationship" with Him. I didn't have a relationship with Him because I never spent time getting to know Him. I used Him when I was in a jam and pushed Him aside the rest of the time. We can only have a relationship with

Jesus when we spend time with Him in prayer and get to know Him by reading Scripture. Our relationship strengthens when we recognize who He is and praise Him for all He has done, and we honor Him with our words and actions.

God desires to have a relationship with you. What a beautiful gift that the Creator of the Universe wants to know you! If that doesn't make you feel special, I don't know what will. This relationship will be the best relationship you will ever have. When you have a genuine relationship with Jesus you are different, your life is different. The relationship is not one-sided and solely about what you can get, rather, it is focused first on how you can serve the will of your Friend. It is only through relationship that we can become who He intended us to be and live a blessed life. A relationship with Him changes everything because your focus changes to *who* really matters, and everything else fades into the background. It is vital that you begin to see Jesus as your Friend and Father whom you can place your trust in. When you begin to understand who God is and what He did for you, you can't help but fall in love with Him.

When I was younger and clearly not as wise, I would run to my friends and family when an issue arose. I spent countless hours complaining and trying to come up with a solution, which often left me no better off. Now when I encounter an issue, I go directly to God. This doesn't mean that a solution magically appears, but being in His presence gives me a sense of peace and comfort. God is the ultimate comforter and provider and focusing on Him will give you the peace you need to see you through any issue. When you focus on God, you don't have to control everything. Build a relationship with Him that is filled with hope, trust, and obedience and through Him everything else will be possible.

Growing a relationship with God affords you the comfort of not having to worry about life. God clearly tells us in the Bibe not to worry about anything. Instead, He says to pray about everything. What are we doing when we pray? We are giving our attention and worries to God because like a good Father, He will take care of us.

> *"Do not worry about anything; instead pray about everything. Tell God what you need, and thank him for all he has done. Then you will experience God's peace which exceeds anything we can understand. His peace will guard your heart and minds as you live in Christ Jesus." (Philippians 4:6–7 NLT)*

How can God tell us not to worry about anything? We live in a world full of things to worry about—war, stock market crashes, our finances, our health, our families, and the list goes on. We are so consumed with worry that we forget about God. Ironically, He is the way to find peace in all situations and is the only One who has the power to move mountains for us. God doesn't say to pray only about the big troubles in your life. He says "everything," and there is only one way to interpret this: it means *all*. He commands us to look to Him for peace in all situations because that is how He takes care of His children.

We live in a society where our focus is often divided. There are many distractions and "things" vying for our attention. The enemy wants us to worry about our circumstances instead of going to God. When we constantly worry about everything under the sun we leave no time for God. This is subtle, yet quite destructive. We have one singular job and that is to focus on cultivating a relationship with God. God is bigger than your biggest problem. When we keep our focus on God, we begin to realize how minor everything else is in comparison.

To grow your relationship with God you will need to have three things in place: a time to pray, a place to pray, and a plan for your prayer time. I suggest making prayer the first thing you do in the morning. It makes sense that you would give God the first moments of your day. Coming to Him first thing in the morning sets the tone for the rest of your day; if you wait until later in the day you run the risk of other things consuming your time. I have designated a chair in my bedroom as my "prayer chair." I wake up, brush my teeth (I can't talk to God with stinky morning breath), and sit in this chair to read my Bible and pray.

Once you begin to know God better, you will be able to discern when He is "talking" to you. God communicates with everyone in different ways. You may hear His voice audibly, receive a thought, or receive a vision. I often feel a nudge from God when there is something I should or shouldn't do. Sometimes we don't hear from God because we are not listening, so it is essential to include some silent time during your prayers so God can speak to you however He chooses.

One morning during my prayer time I saw in my minds eye, "DO NOT GO," in all caps. Because I was not praying about going anywhere, I asked God, "Do not go where?" He responded, "Switzerland." My husband and I were in the process of planning my forty-fifth birthday trip to Switzerland. For a few days I tried to brush this off and continued planning the trip, but I felt unsettled and told my husband that we couldn't go. He thought it was strange, but he knows me well: I will always be obedient when God speaks to me. So we decided to go to Colorado instead—the Switzerland of the United States. As soon as we started planning our trip to Colorado my uneasy feeling subsided and the rest was smooth and easy. I don't know why God told me not to travel to Switzerland—maybe He was protecting us from something or maybe He was testing my obedience. Whatever the case, it didn't matter because I trust Him completely.

I haven't always listened to God, partly because I wasn't sure it was Him and partly because I wanted to exert my will over His, which has never ended well. When I started my business as a life coach, I wanted to gather as much knowledge and information as possible to develop the tools and techniques I needed to really help my clients. Pursuing another certification sounded logical, so I paid the five-hundred-dollar deposit on a meditation instructor course. As it turned out I had little time and the funds to move forward, so I lost my down payment.

The following year, my finances were in better shape, so I purchased another course for almost four thousand dollars. At this point in my spiritual journey I was in the process of getting to know God and His Word, but I was not rooted in His Word yet. As I began taking the course, some of the information resonated with me but other parts didn't feel right. There were a lot of undertones from other religions, but I continued to push forward and ignore my unsettled feelings. Because of these feelings, I sought confirmation that I was doing the right thing. I reached out to my representative at the company and his words were comforting. "I am Christian too and I practice the mediations."

Those words temporarily put my mind at ease, but the tightness in my body persisted until I could no longer deny the feeling anymore. God was telling me that this was not honoring Him. Relieved to have made my decision, I tensed up as I realized that I had missed the date for a refund on the course. Before telling my husband, I attempted to get the refund, but the company stuck with their strict return policy.

After learning that I could not get my money back, I prayed for Alex to receive this information well. Alex had always been supportive, but I felt that I had made an egregious error by not doing my research prior to purchasing the course. Alex was lying in bed relaxing when I broke the news, tears rolling down my face. He listened intently and paused before he responded. "I see how upset this is making you and although I'm not happy we lost all that money because we could've really used it, I believe in you and want you to follow your heart and do what you think is right."

I started crying even harder because I was so grateful for Alex, his kindness, his support, and his understanding. God had softened Alex's heart and opened it to receive this bad news. As I look back on that experience, I see how the enemy was trying to prevent us from having a relationship with God by cunningly dividing our attention with all this new age stuff to heal us, like crystals and Reiki healers. God heals. These modalities strip the glory and power away from God. They make us think that we can heal ourselves through mystical powers not connected to God. This is how evil slowly takes over: by replacing the need for God, by replacing the need for a relationship with Him. It is so subtle that it is easily missed. We all need to make having a relationship with Him a priority.

> *"Let no one deceive you with empty words, for because of such things God's wrath comes on those who are disobedient. Therefore do not be partners with them. For you were once darkness, but now you are light in the Lord. Live as children of light (for the fruit of the light consists in all goodness, righteousness, and truth). Have nothing to do with the fruitless deeds of darkness, but rather expose them. But everything exposed by the light becomes visible—and everything that is illuminated becomes a light. This is why it is said: 'Wake up, sleeper, rise from the dead, and Christ will shine on you.' Be very careful, then, how you live—not as unwise but as wise, making the most of every opportunity, because the days are evil. Therefore do not be foolish, but understand what the Lord's will is." (Ephesians 5:6–9, 11, 13–17 NIV)*

Our relationship with God is our weapon against evil. His light will always cast out the darkness. It is through our relationship with God that we can overcome sin and find peace in this evil and chaotic world.

∾

Prayer

Lord, I desire to grow my relationship with you. Grant me the wisdom to know the difference between what is of the light and what is not. Guide me to seek your strength and wisdom in all situations. Give me the courage to do what is right. Amen.

Reflect

Do you have a relationship with God? How do you know? Make a plan to start spending time with God. Remember to pick a place, time, and a plan for each day. I highly recommend the *You Version Bible* app for daily Bible plans and for their daily "Verse of the Day" videos and prayers.

Laura Lopez-Arenas

When We Trust God

CHAPTER 7

Do I Have to Attend Church?

Church was always on my Sunday list of things to do along with laundry, dishes, and cleaning the bathroom. As you can see, it was quite the fun-filled list. I saw church as a chore. My faith consisted of marking off items on my to-do list. Baptism, communion, confessions, and confirmation: done.

My church upbringing conditioned me to follow the rules that the church established for me. The priest had a relationship with God and that is why I had to go to church. I was unaware that I could have a relationship with God too. For most of my life I followed a church and religion instead of following Jesus. Church should not be something you "have to do," but rather something "you get to do." The job of a church is to help you grow your faith. It is a place where you can surround yourself with other believers who will pray with you and support you. It is a place that you not only receive from, but give back to. Getting involved and serving at church has been one of the biggest blessings in my life. Let's be honest and address the "reason" so many people write off church. I have heard and said all of the following:

- "I don't get anything out of going to church." If you are attending the wrong church and are not putting any effort into being a part of the community, then you most certainly won't get any benefit out of church. You need to be an active member and not just a passive observer. Church is a way to connect to the Word of God and surround yourself with other believers to help you grow spiritually. Church helps set you up for a successful week. You won't grow your faith by just going to church once a week and then forgetting about God for the remainder of the week. It is like eating a healthy meal once a week and thinking you will be healthy regardless of what you eat for the rest of the week. Highly unlikely! The church has so much more to offer than just Sunday service. You can get involved in volunteer opportunities, Life Group activities, Bible Studies, worship nights, and other activities.
- "I don't have to attend church to know God." This is true, but God commands us to honor the Sabbath and go to church. God is practical and has His reasons for this as I mentioned above. He knows that we need a place to feed

our souls. You may or may not find God in a church, but if you know God, you will want to attend church.

- "The Bible is antiquated and not relevant to my life." Yes, there are versions of the Bible that are written in antiquated language. For many years I listened to my priest read from the *King James Bible*. All the "art thou's and cometh's" made me feel confused and disinterested. I had never read the Bible because I could not understand it until I discovered that there are different versions. What?!?! There are translations like the *New Living Testament* (NLT) and the *New International Version* (NIV) that are written in simple language that even children can understand. Find a church that uses a version of the Bible you understand and that the pastor can help you relate to your life. I love reading the Bible now! There is more drama in the Bible than any soap opera you can find on your streaming platforms. The pages are filled with hope, trust, encouragement, and more. You will find average people like yourself who failed by their own volition and yet triumphed through God's mercy and power.
- "Church is just filled with hypocrites." There are some hypocrites at church. My pastor's response to this comment is, "There is room for another." (Chuckle.) Don't let those people deter you from attending church. Remember, people might seem like hypocrites, but they are really in the process of sanctification. They are growing and changing, but still susceptible to sin. Sometimes Christians don't always represent God in the most appropriate way, but don't hold that against God.

They are working on becoming more like God and less like themselves.

I will tell you what church is definitely full of: sinners. We are all sinners; none of us are perfect. We are all trying to do our best. Even though I know and love God, I still mess up. Being flawed doesn't mean you are not a Christian, it means you are a human—a human who needs God's guidance and love.

For better or worse, we tend to become like the people we spend time with. We talk like them, think like them, and act like them. If you hang out with a gang, you become a gang member. If you hang out with gossipy soccer moms, you become a gossipy soccer mom. We conform to the environment we live in. For a long time, I was stubborn and thought I knew better than everyone else. I would roll my eyes at people who said I needed to attend church. My response was always the same: I don't need a church to be connected to God. He can be in many places at once and He can be with me anywhere. This is true. There is no place that God's love can't reach you.

But church is not for God's benefit, rather, it is for our benefit. Church is a community that fills our need to feel like we belong. We can find belonging either in a church or with groups that might not care for us. There are negative communities that will drag you down and lead you to destruction, but a church is a positive community that lifts you up and helps you transform your life. It is for you to decide what type of community you want to participate in.

Church is a place where you can surround yourself with people who have similar goals and dreams. These people will encourage and support you and pray with you when times are tough. A church family will speak life over you and share the Word of God. Finding a church to call home is essential to your spiritual growth.

For most of my life I went to a Catholic church, but when I moved to Texas I began attending a Christian non-denominational church. The first time I attended I felt weird and awkward. The church looked like a convention hall with a massive stage and rows of chairs. No pews, relics, ornate crosses, statues of saints, or stained-glass windows. As if that wasn't strange enough, a band played, and singers bounced on the stage and sang relatable modern songs that I wanted to dance to. People were singing and throwing their hands in the air and clapping. Then, to top it off, the pastor wasn't a priest. He was dressed in normal clothes and read verses that I could understand and relate to, and I didn't have to kneel, sit, stand, and repeat. My mind was blown and I was confused. I thought these were probably the cults my mother warned me about. Kidding! I had to let go of what I thought church *should* be to make room for the possibility of what church *could* be.

For the first few months, Alex and I attended service and darted out of the church afterward so no one would engage with us. We were still a little weirded out by all the happy, worshipping people, but we liked the powerful message. Each week on our way home we talked about the message and discussed how it was applicable to our lives. God was moving us and we could feel the change brewing inside.

I decided that I wanted and needed more. Around month seven I felt this push to get more involved in the church. Alex was already going to church every week, which was a huge step for him, and I was worried that if I pushed too hard he would do the opposite of what I wanted. I didn't really know where to go or how to start, so I tried to join some Life Group activities to get involved and meet people, but the meeting times were not conducive to my schedule.. Here is where the power of intention plays a role. God saw my intention and genuine heart. I was making an effort to follow His will and get more involved. Because of that, He made a way.

One Sunday we arrived at service early and Alex went to the restroom. While I was standing outside, the pastor's wife stopped and asked me if we had met. Being slightly judgmental, I thought, "Yes, this is the third time we are meeting, thanks for paying attention." Quickly remembering where I was, I gave her some grace because I had never had a proper conversation with her. At the time I didn't recognize it, but I do now. The enemy was using offense to prevent me from having a conversation with her that God had put in place.

She initiated a conversation while I waited for Alex to return. We talked about ways to get more involved in the church and how hard it could be with busy schedules. It turned out that she was in charge of one of the service teams and offered Alex and I the opportunity to serve. I knew that God was answering my prayers and guiding us to an opportunity to get more involved in the church. My excitement quickly faded when Alex returned: he would never agree to spending two and half hours in the church each week. As he listened, he turned to me and nodded in agreement. My heart was about to burst with gratitude for God having a hand in this interaction.

It has been over two years since we started volunteering. We have a beautiful Life Group that we meet with every other week, and those couples have become our friends. I organize volunteer opportunities at church, and recently Alex and I were asked to lead our group's weekly morning huddle by discussing faith. Attending church is as automatic now as breathing air. It is something we want to do and that we look forward to each week. If we miss a week, we feel like something is missing. Those individuals have become our family, and I have never experienced anything like this in my life.

Church doesn't have to be a chore. Find a church you feel connected to and get involved. Take advantage of all the church has to offer for spiritual growth. Don't just attend service and go home. Get involved and become invested in the church's mission. Surround yourself with other believers that are further along on their spiritual journey than you are so you can learn from them. Church is not a one-size-fits-all. Pray that God will lead you to a church that will help you grow and use your God-given talents.

The church I belong to now looks very different from the church I belonged to as a child. Church is no longer an obligation, it's a passion. It is something I look forward to doing each week with my husband. It is my priority on Sunday. I choose God every day, but especially on Sundays.

Prayer

Father, you know what is best for me. Guide me to a church that will support me in my efforts to grow my faith and deepen my relationship with you. Show me where I can use my talents to serve you and your people. Amen.

Reflect

What has your experience been with attending church? Do you have a church that you feel connected to?

When We Trust God

CHAPTER 8

Sharing the Good News

When I first heard someone tell me to share the Good News, I wondered what news they were referring to and why it is so good. This Good News is that Jesus is our Savior and God sent His only Son to earth to teach us about love and mercy and to give us salvation. Jesus was fully man and fully God. He made a profound impact on the lives of those he met during those times, but His existence made an even bigger impact for future generations.

> *"For God so loved the world that he gave his one and only Son, that whoever believes in him will not perish but have eternal life." (John 3:16 NIV)*

In the Old Testament, people had to partake in sacrifices to atone for their sins. This was a frequent practice so that they would be made acceptable to the Lord. When Jesus laid down His life for mankind, he became the final and ultimate sacrifice. Jesus came to earth so that we may be forgiven, and His death paid the price for all sins of future generations. You can know this fact, but not be saved. Being saved means accepting Jesus as your only Lord and Savior. It means acknowledging what He did and turning away from your sins. It is by His blood that our sins are wiped away and we are made clean.

Now this is news I want to share with everyone! This means that you will have eternal life in Christ. It means that you will be accepted into His family and Kingdom. But there are not just eternal benefits. Truly knowing God has the power to transform you and your life. God's love and mercy have the power to renew you, to take all the pain and mistakes of your past and give them purpose. He will help you overcome obstacles that didn't seem humanly possible to resolve. He will restore health and relationships. Peter wrote about a great peace that we can experience even in awful situations. Despite being in prison, Peter rejoices. How is this possible? It is only possible through God.

> *"I rejoiced greatly in the Lord that at last you renewed your concern for me. Indeed, you were concerned, but you had no opportunity to show it. I am not saying this because I am in need, for I have learned to be content whatever the circumstances. I know what it is to be in need, and I know what it is to have plenty. I have*

learned the secret of being content in any and every situation, whether well fed or hungry, whether living in plenty or in want. I can do all this through him who gives me strength." (Philippians 4:10-13 NIV)

This is such a beautiful gift that we need to share it with others and not just rely on preachers. I was always under the misconception that the church held sole responsibility for bringing people to God. After examining my story of transformation and witnessing the stories of others, I saw how none of those individuals found God because of church. I found God in the people I encountered in my everyday life. It was their wisdom and guidance that pointed me toward God.

One day, when I was a child, there was a knock at the door and I darted down the stairs to answer it. When I heard my mom yell, "Don't answer the door!" I became scared, backed away, and crept quietly back upstairs, worried that there was a "bad man" at the door. I turned to my mom for answers, and she put her hands to her lips and pointed at the door. "Jehovah's Witnesses."

This kind of thing happened often with various religious evangelists. Because of my mom's reaction to them, I began to think that this behavior was not normal and very strange. I formed this idea that preaching God to others was wrong. This idea couldn't be further from the truth. Many times in the Bible, God instructs his disciples to go out and share the gospel.

"He said to them, 'Go into all the world and preach the gospel to all creation.'" (Mark 16:15 NIV)

"Preach the word; be prepared in season and out of season; correct, rebuke and encourage—with great patience and careful instruction." (2 Timothy 4:2 NIV)

God calls everyone to share the Good News. We lead by example so that people can see the light of God shining within us. Share your story and be a witness for the transformative power that God offers everyone through His love and mercy. Invite friends, family members, and strangers to church. Keep inviting them even if they are not receptive at first.

My husband was one of those people who wanted nothing to do with church or religion. I totally understood why he felt the way he did, but I had to make him see the God I know. At first, I tried convincing him of the truth, which generally ended up in an argument. Frustrated, I eventually gave up because my words were causing more trouble than good. Instead, I let my actions speak for themselves. As he began to notice subtle changes in me, his curiosity was sparked. I focused on my relationship with God and kept Alex in my prayers. I knew I was onto something when he said to me, "I want what you have." He didn't exactly know what he was asking for, but knew he wanted the trust, peace, and hope that I exuded.

After I became born again in Christ, my sister Jennifer started acting a little funny. She would ask me if something was wrong because of the type of posts I was sharing on social media. She called me a Holy Roller and questioned the church I was attending. She noticed something was different about me and found it strange and worrisome. I completely understood why she reacted this way because we were raised in the same house. I accepted that she didn't have to agree with me or understand what was going on. It took months before she went from wondering what was wrong with me to asking what was right with me. Her curiosity was an invitation to share God. At first it was a bit of a struggle to undo some of the false teachings we had both received at a young age. The Bible was a huge help, as I would send her verses to back up my words. I would often chuckle when I shared a Biblical truth with her. She would kindly say, "I don't know if I agree." My response was always the same: "I am not giving you my opinion, I am quoting the truths from the Bible." Eventually she began to understand. Her transformation was, and continues to be, beautiful to witness. She has restored her faith, prays every morning, and is working on her relationship with God. This would not have happened if I had kept my relationship with God to myself. As a Christian, it is your job to share the Good News and promote the Kingdom of God on earth.

Prayer

Lord, show me opportunities to share your Good News with others. Help me to be bold as I share my witness to your love and mercy. Help me to be radiant, so that others can see your light within me. Amen.

Reflect

Do you find it easy or difficult to share your faith and why? What is your testimony for God?

When We Trust God

CHAPTER 9

Creating a Wedge

I once heard someone close to me say, "I'd rather be friends with an atheist who is doing the right thing than be friends with a Christian who is a hypocrite." As Christians, we need to be careful not to deter people from following God. Unfortunately, I have seen this play out repeatedly on social media and in the news. Christians who are supposed to be sharing the Good News to bring people to God are having the opposite effect. Many Christians are creating a wedge between God and mankind—we are supposed to be representatives for God on earth. We are here to help people find salvation, not to be the reason they turn their backs on God. Our behavior has eternal effects. Don't be the reason someone decides God is not the way.

Christians, churches, and religious leaders do not always appropriately represent our loving God. Sometimes, their actions and words contradict who God is. They are supposed to be a representative for God, but they are not perfect and can make mistakes. Only God is perfect—He is the same yesterday, today, and tomorrow. If you judge God based on religion and human beings, you will be disappointed and offended every time. Let's make a promise not to judge God based on the actions of others. Even though Christians have given their lives to Christ, they are still humans who make mistakes and are not capable of being perfect.

> *"For everyone has sinned; we all fall short of God's glorious standard." (Romans 3:23 NLT)*

Being a Christian means leaning on God in your weakness and asking Him for help to overcome sin. It is God's power that gives Christians the strength to triumph through their weaknesses. Knowing Jesus makes us better. Because we live in this dark world, we will always be subject to sin that makes all humans flawed.

Some people claim to be Christian, but sadly do not act or speak in a Christ-like manner. This statement is a tough one for me because I was that person for a good portion of my life. It hurts to think that people might have been judging God based on my actions. I was not the poster child for living a faith-filled life. Even worse are pastors or priests that partake in scandalous behavior. There are scandals in the news about pastors cheating on their wives and stealing from the church.

I have heard countless stories over the years of the church conducting themselves in a way that was off-putting. This creates resentment and distrust in the church, but even more bothersome, it creates a lack of trust in God. Get to know your Creator who loves and adores you. Don't let the sin of man separate you from your Father. Writing that sentence brought me to tears for two reasons: I am overjoyed that I now love and know God, yet I am sad that there are some people who have not experienced his mercy and love.

It took many years to get Alex to attend church and start living a faith-filled life. We finally found a church to call home, and Alex was in a good place, growing his faith and opening up to those around him. One day, he had an off-putting experience with someone at church. He was upset and asked me to help him calm down. I was concerned that this incident would make him revert to his old ways of thinking about the church. To my surprise, Alex was hurt, yet logical. We talked about it, and he decided not to let anyone come between him and God. Together we prayed that God might enter his heart and make him understand why he had acted the way he did, and that he would not do it again. When you are committed to your faith and relationship with God, you do not allow any obstacles to stand in your way.

Only Christ is perfect. Everyone else is just trying to do their best. Humans are not perfect and that is why we need God's grace. In turn, we must offer grace to others. That means being understanding when someone acts foolish. We are all spiritual beings trying to navigate in a place that is not our home. It is challenging and we often make mistakes. Please do not determine whether you want to follow Christ based on people, a church, or a popular pastor. Follow Jesus because of who He is and what He has already done for you on the cross. Don't let anyone come between you and having a relationship with Him.

∼

Prayer

Lord, help me to focus on you and your perfect love. Do not let the sin of man distract me from accepting salvation. Show me opportunities to love your children as you love me. Give me the wisdom and guidance to be a light for others and to represent you to the best of my ability. Amen.

Reflect

Have you ever had an experience that caused you to separate from the church and God? Ask God for help to move past this experience so that you can experience His love.

When We Trust God

Laura Lopez-Arenas

CHAPTER 10

The Joyful Giver

With coffee and two pastries in hand, Alex and I headed off to a local soup kitchen. We had volunteered before, but today was special because we were meeting some of our church family there. On our way to the food pantry Alex noticed a homeless man holding a cardboard sign that read "I'm hungry." Without hesitating, he rolled down the window and waved the man over. The man's eyes widened, and a huge smile lit his face as Alex offered him a muffin. With a grateful heart, the man repeatedly thanked us for the food and returned to his corner post. As we waited for the light to turn green we witnessed the man's reaction as he took that first bite. He smiled broadly and gave us a thumbs up and nodded incessantly with enjoyment. His joy fed our spirits.

When we arrived at the soup kitchen, the coordinator made an announcement that they were in dire need of many sandwiches for the day. Their need had almost doubled, and her voice was full of doubt that we could produce four thousand eight hundred sandwiches during our shift. That doubt lit a fire under the volunteers. In addition to feeding three hundred and ninety people that afternoon, we made five thousand four hundred and seventy-one sandwiches—an all-time record! The coordinator was shocked that we had made so many sandwiches and was overjoyed by the outcome. She later told me that she had prayed to God that He would send her a productive group. Because God is extraordinary, we didn't just meet the goal, but well surpassed it.

During this miracle, God was busy at work cultivating another miracle. I was pulled off sandwich duty to help another volunteer prepare raw chicken legs and thighs for cooking. (I am a vegetarian, so this was borderline torture for me.) The man told me that serving at the soup kitchen was his way of repaying the shelter for providing he and his wife and infant with food and shelter. He also told me that his car was broken and he had the part to fix it, but couldn't afford the labor. Normally, I would have offered encouraging words and prayers, but God gently told me that this was not sufficient and I had to get involved.

I didn't want to give the man hope only to let him down if I couldn't help, but I trusted that if God was calling me to offer assistance, then He would make a way. Sure enough, the next day at church, we did a recap of our volunteer experience and I learned that a nice guy at church was a mechanic. The following weekend he replaced the part and tuned up the car. God is good and trustworthy. His love and care never ceases to amaze me.

When we are obedient and serve God, it is incredible what God can make happen. He used this one event to bless many. Generally, I find that I gain much more from giving than receiving. When we give from the heart and not out of obligation, God smiles.

> *"Each of you should give what you have decided in your heart to give, not reluctantly or under compulsion, for God loves a cheerful giver." (2 Corinthians 9:7–8 NIV)*

Giving can come in many forms. You can give your time, talents, and finances. God does not require you to donate to the poor, sick, homeless, hungry, etc. However, He loves when we care for others. If God has blessed you, use your blessings to bless someone else.

> *"The generous will find themselves blessed, for they share their food with the poor." (Proverbs 22:9 NIV)*

God sees your generous acts of giving to those in need. When you care for His people, He takes those acts very personally and it is as if you are doing them directly for God.

> *"And the King will say, I tell you the truth, whatever you did for one of the least of these brothers and sisters of mine, you did for me." (Matthew 25:40 NIV)*

The second kind of giving is called tithing and this is not optional. This is when you give ten percent of your income to the church. Please don't close this book. I sense your eyes rolling and completely understand your potential annoyance and disregard.

Even after I surrendered my life to God, I was still not tithing. For a while I felt guilty about it, but a friend told me that you will know when it's the right time to tithe. God doesn't want you to give out of guilt, but rather with a joyful heart. Her words lifted my burden, and rather than feeling guilty I prayed for God to give me the desire to be a joyful giver. At this point I was tithing on my income, but my husband was not ready to tithe on his. I couldn't force him into this choice. It had to be by his own volition. This was a happy medium solution for us in the interim.

Giving to those in need might come easily to you, but giving to the church might be a hard no. I know what you are thinking and how you are feeling because my husband and I had those same sentiments. In case you don't believe me, here is a list of our thoughts:

- The church is so corrupt; I am not donating my hard-earned money to them.
- I don't even know what they are doing with my money. I'll bet the pastor is living a good life off the congregation's donations. That is probably how he obtained that nice beach home.
- The Bible doesn't say I have to donate to the church. (Actually, it does.)

> *"Honor the Lord with your wealth, with the first fruits of all your crops; then your barn will be filled to overflowing, and your vats will brim over with new wine." (Proverbs 3:9–10 NIV)*

- Here comes that basket again, what can I scrounge up out of my purse? Two dollars and fifty cents—perfect!
- I am living paycheck to paycheck and have tons of debt; God understands that I don't have the money to give right now.

Now that we have that out of the way, let's talk about giving. Before I was saved I would rummage through my bag for a few crumpled singles, totally bypassing the crisp twenty in my wallet. I gave out of obligation, not out of joy. Looking back, I am embarrassed that is all I thought God deserved. I was giving Him my leftovers! In the Old Testament, God would not accept an offering that was defective, only perfect gifts. It is easy to give away "something" that is defective or less valuable, but it is much harder to give away "things of value." In the following verse, we see how God demands more.

> *"Give Aaron and his sons and all the Israelites these instructions, which apply both to native Israelites and to the foreigners living among you. If you present a gift as a burnt offering to the Lord, whether it is to fulfill a vow or is a voluntary offering, you will be accepted only if your offering is a male animal with no defects. It may be a bull, a ram, or a male goat. Do not present*

an animal with defects, because the Lord will not accept it on your behalf." (Leviticus 22:18-20 NLT)

In this next verse, a woman gave less than all the rich men, but it was all she had. Her donation was greater because her need for the money was greater. The rich men gave only a drop of water from their full buckets.

"Jesus looked up and saw rich men putting their money into the money box in the house of God. He saw a poor woman whose husband had died. She put in two very small pieces of money. He said, 'I tell you the truth, this poor woman has put in more than all of them. For they have put in a little of the money they had no need for. She is very poor and has put in all she had. She has put in what she needed for her own living.'" (Luke 21:1–4 NLV)

My husband Alex and I have found Jesus: it was our faith and trust in the Lord that opened our minds and hearts to giving to the church. At first, my heart was open to giving—Alex needed to catch up. We had become regulars at church and Alex was growing and changing, but he was not ready to open his wallet yet. One Sunday I told him I was ready to start giving and his eyes widened in disbelief as I placed a twenty-dollar bill in the giving envelope.

For the next few months, I made a monthly donation of fifty dollars. Since I used to give a few singles each week, fifty dollars was a lot to me, but I knew in my heart that I could do more. The next month I gave one hundred dollars. I had mixed emotions about it. I was happy to give to the church, but felt guilty because I was doing this behind my husband's back. After a few months I felt justified because I had decided I wasn't going to let anyone interfere with my walk with God. My guilt prompted me to pray for God to open Alex's heart to giving. Then, during an argument one Sunday, my secret was exposed. Alex was annoyed but he quickly got over it. He wanted to start giving. It was tough for him, but after another week of talking and debating, he agreed to give two hundred dollars each month. This was a huge step in the right direction, but still not considered tithing.

After donating for a few months, the annual appeal arrived and I followed my heart—I wanted to go big and show God that I loved and trusted Him. I wanted Him to know I could be bold for Him. I took a deep breath and asked Alex if we could contribute. My request was met with a head tilt, an eye roll, and a smirk. He didn't say no, so I knew there was hope. After pleading my case he finally said he would think about it. On the day we needed to make the decision to contribute to the annual appeal, I felt that God was telling me Alex and I had to agree on an amount. I said three thousand and Alex said two, so we compromised and met halfway.

Almost another year went by and we were still not tithing. I had mentioned increasing our monthly contribution, but Alex was not having it. Finally, after much convincing and a lot of praying, Alex agreed to let me tithe on my salary. Although we are still not tithing on our total income, I know that God sees my heart and that we are moving toward the full ten percent.

By the way, this is the only area that God allows you to test Him. Give God what is due to Him and see how He blesses your health, your finances, your children, your relationships, and more.

> *"Should people cheat God? Yet you have cheated me! But you ask, 'What do you mean? When did we ever cheat you? You have cheated me of the tithes and offerings due to me. You are under a curse, for your whole nation has been cheating me. Bring all the tithes into the storehouse so there will be enough food in my Temple.' 'If you do,' says the Lord of Heaven's Armies, 'I will open the windows of heaven for you. I will pour out a blessing so great you won't have enough room to take it in! Try it! Put me to the test!'" (Malachi 3:8–10 NLT)*

People have told me that I'm crazy for donating all that money to the church, but I'm not offended because I would have said that myself a few years ago. Give what you can with a genuine, joyful heart and pray for God to help you get to a place where tithing is natural and easy.

Prayer

Lord, help me to be a generous and joyful giver. Open up opportunities for me to share the blessings that you have given me. Show me how I can use my time, money, talents, and resources to be a blessing to others. Amen.

Reflect

What is holding you back from being a joyful giver? How can you use your talents to serve others?

Laura Lopez-Arenas

CHAPTER 11

Speaking Life

God made you and He doesn't make mistakes. You were beautifully and wonderfully created.

> *"For you created my innermost being; you knit me together in my mother's womb. I praise you because I am fearfully and wonderfully made; your works are wonderful and I know them full well." (Psalms 139:13–14 NIV)*

When we talk badly about ourselves and others we are condemning God's work and not praising Him for His creations. That is why talking badly about yourself and others is so detrimental.

> *"For we are God's handiwork created through Christ Jesus to do good works which God prepared in advance for us to do." (Ephesians 2:10 NIV)*

We are God's handiwork, and we should talk to ourselves and others as if we know that we are a splendid masterpiece created by the most famous Artist.

There is power in our words. I am sure most of you have heard this statement before. Our words either lift others up or tear them down. They give encouragement, love, and healing, or cause pain and suffering. What are your words conveying to yourself and others?

Let's take this secular statement and examine it from a spiritual perspective. Speaking life equals speaking God's truths. When we speak life over others we are confirming that what God says is true. Take a look at these Bible verses and let the words settle in for a moment.

> *"A good man brings good things out of the good stored up in his heart, and an evil man brings evil things out of the evil stored up in his heart. For the mouth speaks what the heart is full of." (Luke 6:45 NIV)*

> *"You brood of vipers, how can you who are evil say anything good? For the mouth speaks what the heart is full of. A good man brings good things out of the good stored up in him, and an evil man brings evil things out of the evil stored up in him. But I tell you that everyone will have to give account on the day of judgment for*

every empty word they have spoken. For by your words you will be acquitted, and by your words you will be condemned."(Matthew 12:34–37 NIV)

Basically, what comes out of your mouth reflects what is in your heart. It is reflective of your emotions, thoughts, and experiences. There is intention behind everything we say. Are your words meant to be hurtful or uplifting? Do they provide comfort or inflict pain? The words we speak are a good indicator of where we are in our spiritual lives.

I knew that I was growing spiritually when cursing felt ugly to me. It left a bad taste in my mouth and hurt my heart. And negative words extend beyond just cursing. Gossiping, complaining, and judgment are just as bad. Sometimes we might not realize the impact of our words: our negative words hurt others, as well as ourselves. Essentially, our speech has the power to bring life or death to all those who hear it.

It is only through speaking life that we can cultivate change, growth, and power. Speaking life over others has the power to change circumstances and transform our minds and hearts. Don't focus on what you don't like about others, but rather see them as God sees them—wonderfully made and created for a purpose. When we can see others as God sees them, it is easier to speak words of encouragement. God tells us that we will be condemned for our words and our words paint a good picture about the life we are living.

I once heard that a life surrendered to God will produce speech full of grace, mercy, love, and power. How different would the world look? What would our relationships be like if we all spoke out of love and mercy? The great news is that God created us to have qualities that would facilitate this type of speech. Use your God-given power to produce good fruit.

> *"For God has not given us a spirit of fear and timidity, but of power, love, and self-discipline." (2 Timothy 1:7 NLT)*

I want to share some practical tips to help you harness your power, love, and self-discipline. Be patient and kind to yourself. You need to rewire how you think and speak, which will take time and effort. This is scientific, but I am not going to get into the research. Remember that if you have people in your life who do not speak life, it will be challenging to speak life to them when they are not reciprocating, but stay strong and pray.

- Pray: Most importantly, pray continually. Connecting with God will assist you to access the words to build others up and provide you with the strength you need to fight the urge to be hurtful. It can be as simple as, "Lord, help me use words that lift others up. Search my heart and show me how to change."
- Speak God's truths: There is power in God's words. The Word of God is tangible evidence of His presence. Too often we find it easier to believe the lies of the enemy than the truths of God. Use Scripture as your armor. Speak verses over yourself and those around you.

- Pause and breathe: Too often we speak without thinking. We react to a person or event from an emotional place and our mouths revert to autopilot. Once it is too late, we realize that we regret the words that poured out of our mouths. This is a lack of self-control, but we know that God equipped us with what we need to exhibit discipline. When an incident occurs, instead of reacting, pause and take several deeps breaths.

As you begin to align yourself with God's words, you will see your life and your relationships transform. There is power in the words of the Bible. Use them to speak love and light into this dark world.

Prayer

Lord, search my heart and show me how my words offend you. Give me a speech filled with love, compassion, kindness, and mercy. Give me the wisdom to know what to say. Guard my tongue against sinful words. Amen.

Reflect

Make a list of the words you speak throughout the day. This is a good way to take inventory as to whether you are speaking life or death. Label each phrase with a "D" for speaking death or an "L for speaking Life. What areas of your life are you not speaking life into? How can you change that?

When We Trust God

CHAPTER 12

The Power of God

Somewhere, somehow, we have learned to be fearful and worrisome. Social media and the news perpetuate anxiety and fear. We take the bait and become trapped in anxiety and consumed by our thoughts and emotions, which creates a wall separating us from God. The enemy uses fear as a weapon to sever our connection with God. When we are worrying we are telling God that we don't trust Him, and the enemy wins.

Despite the looming fear of war, natural disasters, political unrest, increased crime, and more, Christians can find comfort in knowing that God is in charge, and that He alone has overcome evil. As we keep our focus on Him, He provides us with peace. God is our source for everything good. If we are to live well, we must stay connected to our Source.

> *"For you will keep in perfect peace all who trust in you, all those thoughts are fixed on you." (Isaiah 26:3 NLT)*

> *"Yes, I am the vine and you are the branches. Those who remain in me and I in them will produce much fruit. For apart from me, you can do nothing." (John 5:15 NLT)*

If anxiety and fear are plaguing you, then you have allowed these emotions to be bigger than God. If we shift our perspective and begin to praise God in all situations instead of allowing anxiety to consume us, fear will lose its grip. We already have everything we need to do this. However, we must learn how to use what God gave us to create habits that promote emotional wellness. God gave us the power and tools we need to accomplish this. He did not create us to be fearful and timid. Rather, He gave us a spirit with the ability to overcome.

> *"For God has not given us a spirit of fear and timidity, but of power, love, and self-discipline." (2 Timothy 1:7 NLT)*

I have heard many people talk about these innate qualities and refer to the provider as the Source, the Universe, and Love. They believe in something, but seem hesitant to call Him God. There is one God who made the heavens and the earth and everything in it. Don't strip God of His glory and praise. These tools were given to you by God and He alone has the power we need to overcome trials and tribulations.

Whenever I encountered an issue in my life my mom would say, "pray about it," causing me to brush her off. I knew there was validity in her words, but praying seemed laborious to me and even pointless at times. I believed in Him, but I didn't exactly trust Him because I lacked a relationship with Him. Now that I pray every day and often pray throughout the day, prayer seems so natural and logical. It really goes deeper than prayer—it is about connection and relationship. When you are connected to God, you are in contact with the one true source of love. When you take your mind off your issues and put your trust in God, you are letting Him know that you trust Him, that He alone is your comforter, your provider, your rock, your foundation, your peace. It is a simple equation: Problem + Prayer = Peace.

The answer to everything is God. Let's try this:

- Question: What do I do if I have problems in my marriage? Answer: God
- Question: What do I do if I can't beat this addiction? Answer: God
- Question: What do I do if I need to heal from the past? Answer: God

Are you getting my point? That is not to say we don't need doctors, therapists, medicine, and counselors. But make sure that God is the center of your decision on which therapist to see or which medicine would be best to take. Trust in Him to be the filter that your entire life flows through.

> *"Trust in the Lord your God with all your heart and do not lean on your own understanding. Seek His will in all you do and He will show you which path to take." (Proverbs 3:5–6 NLT)*

God has given us powerful "tools" to assist us in creating good spiritual, mental, and emotional health: prayer, Scripture, breath, and thoughts and emotions.

- Prayer: Prayer is how we communicate with God. During prayer, we talk to God and listen for His wisdom and guidance. Being connected to God allows us to have more peace in our lives and less fear. During prayer we are praising God and, when we are grateful, fear and anxiety cannot co-exist.

> *"Always be joyful. Never stop praying." (1 Thessalonians 5:16–17 NLT)*

- Scripture: Reading the Word of God is like having an owner's manual for living. We look to the Bible for truth, guidance, comfort, peace, and mercy. The Bible also allows us to get to know God better and understand how to navigate this life.

> *"All Scripture is inspired by God and is useful to teach us what is true and to make us realize what is wrong in*

our lives. It corrects us when we are wrong and teaches us to do what is right. God uses it to prepare and equip his people to do every good work." (2 Timothy 3:16-17 NLT)

- Breath: We probably take breathing for granted because it occurs without thinking. However, when we do think about it we realize that it is God's breath that runs through our bodies and gives us life.

"Then the Lord God formed the man from the dust of the ground. He breathed the breath of life into the man's nostrils, and the man became a living person." (Genesis 2:7 NLT)

- Feelings/thoughts: Our thoughts and emotions are powerful. They can either harm us or we can learn how to use them for our betterment. We either control them or they control us.

"And now, dear brothers and sisters, one final thing. Fix your thoughts on what is true, and honorable, and right, and pure, and lovely, and admirable. Think about things that are excellent and worthy of praise." (Philippians 4:8 NLT)

During my journey I learned about a company called the HeartMath Institute, which created research-based techniques to improve heart coherence. When we are in a more coherent space, we can reduce stress and anxiety, think with more clarity, improve resilience, make better choices, be more patient, and more. Our hearts play a larger role than just pumping blood throughout our bodies. The HeartMath Institute has done extensive research in this area. Please visit heartmath.org to view their research studies.

Being a certified HeartMath trainer has given me many tools to share with others. I would like to teach you a simple technique created by the HeartMath Institute and then take it a step further and connect it to God. The Quick Coherence® Technique[2] is deceptively simple, but abundantly powerful. Here are the two steps in this technique:

1. Focus your attention in the area of the heart. Imagine your breath is flowing in and out of your heart or chest area, breathing a little slower and deeper than usual. Find an easy rhythm that's comfortable.
2. As you continue heart-focused breathing, make a sincere attempt to experience a regenerative feeling such as appreciation or care for someone or something in your life.

Note that The Quick Coherence Technique was developed by HeartMath and is a registered trademark of HeartMath. HeartMath is a registered trademark of Quantum Intech, Inc. For all HeartMath trademarks, go to heartmath.com/trademarks.

---

[2] McCraty, Rollin, Science of the Heart, *Exploring the Role of the Heart in Human Performance Volume 2*, HeartMath® Institute, 2015, page 174, www.heartmath.org

Although the HeartMath Institute's techniques are for a secular audience, I have been able to see their connection between God and science. In step one, we are instructed to focus on the heart. God tells us the importance of our hearts in Proverbs. Actually, it is mentioned close to one thousand times across various books in the Bible.

> *"Guard your heart above all else, for it determines the course of your life." (Proverbs 4:23 NLT)*

The second step is to breathe. It is this slow, deeply controlled breath that can change physiology by balancing the autonomic nervous system. It is the breath of God that gives us this power. There is power in the breath because His breath flows through our lungs.

> *"For the Spirit of God had made me, and the breath of the Almighty gives me life" (Job 33:4 NLT)*

In the second step we are also told to think about and feel renewing emotions. At any given moment we have the ability to decide how we feel and what we think. We do not need to be prisoners of our surroundings and allow them to dictate how we feel. God instructs us in this next verse to watch our thinking.

> *"And now, dear brothers and sisters, one final thing. Fix your thoughts on what is true, and honorable, and right, and pure, and lovely, and admirable. Think about things*

that are excellent and worthy of praise." (Philippians 4:8 NLT)

Now let's tie it all together. We have the power through God to be in control of how feel, think, and react. The heart and breath are powerful tools according to Scripture and science. Scripture can calm us, and give us hope and peace. It gives us the confidence we need to overcome our struggles and renews our minds, bodies, and spirits.

Once you have moved these feelings of renewal into your heart, let's add the Word of God by practicing a breath prayer. As you inhale, repeat to yourself, "The Lord is my Shepard." On the exhale, say to yourself, "I have all that I need." Repeat this five to ten times while maintaining a steady, slow, controlled breath. Four to five seconds on the inhale and exhale is a good pace, but do what is comfortable for you. Practice the Quick Coherence Technique combined with a Bible verse to start your day, and throughout your day.

Prayer

Father, thank you for providing me with everything I need to navigate my time on earth. I know that you are bigger than any problem or worldly circumstance I have. Help me to have faith when I am fearful. Teach me how to trust you always. Amen.

Reflect

How can you use what God already gave you to make some of your concerns better? Do you trust that God alone can solve your problems?

Laura Lopez-Arenas

CHAPTER 13

Our Extraordinary God

During my divorce from my first husband I simply prayed for peace in my life. My life had been turned upside down during our marriage and every day felt like I was living on a battlefield plagued by anger and anxiety. I took full ownership for the mess I had made of my life because I hadn't listened to God when He told me not to marry this man. I had been fine with being broke, never getting married again, or never owning another home. Every time I prayed, I begged for the strength to overcome my situation and to finally have peace. Basically, I was telling God that I was completely fine with having a mediocre life after divorce. Part of me thought that was all I deserved. After all, this was my fault. Another part of me didn't want to push it and ask God for too much.

Recovering from divorce was already a huge ask considering my circumstances.

At that time I didn't really know Jesus, because if I had, I would have known that He doesn't do mediocre. He is a God of abundance! It was impossible for me to see a way out of my situation, never mind the beautiful life God was waiting to bless me with. The word mediocre is foreign to God because by his nature, he is divine, all knowing, all powerful, majestic, and miraculous—anything but mediocre.

As a child of the Most High God, we rest in a place of abundant love. With that love comes unimaginable blessings. As I think back, I can picture God looking down at me, chuckling at my simpleness, anticipating the time when he would do such spectacular things in my life that I would be left in awe of His love and mercy. My story makes me think of the Prodigal Son. I am sure that many of you can relate to this story.

> *"Jesus continued: There was a man who had two sons. The younger one said to his father, 'Father, give me my share of the estate.' So he divided his property between them. Not long after that, the younger son got together all he had, set off for a distant country and there squandered his wealth in wild living. After he had spent everything, there was a severe famine in that whole country, and he began to be in need. So he went and hired himself out to a citizen of that country, who sent him to his fields to feed pigs. He longed to fill his stomach with the pods that the pigs were eating, but no one gave him anything. When he came to his senses, he said, 'How many of my father's hired servants have food to spare, and here I*

am starving to death! I will set out and go back to my father and say to him: 'Father, I have sinned against heaven and against you. I am no longer worthy to be called your son; make me like one of your hired servants.' So he got up and went to his father. But while he was still a long way off, his father saw him and was filled with compassion for him; he ran to his son, threw his arms around him and kissed him. The son said to him, 'Father, I have sinned against heaven and against you. I am no longer worthy to be called your son.' But the father said to his servants, 'Quick! Bring the best robe and put it on him. Put a ring on his finger and sandals on his feet. Bring the fattened calf and kill it. Let's have a feast and celebrate. For this son of mine was dead and is alive again; he was lost and is found.' So they began to celebrate. Meanwhile, the older son was in the field. When he came near the house, he heard music and dancing. So he called one of the servants and asked him what was going on. 'Your brother has come,' he replied, 'and your father has killed the fattened calf because he has him back safe and sound.' The older brother became angry and refused to go in. So his father went out and pleaded with him. But he answered his father, 'Look! All these years I've been slaving for you and never disobeyed your orders. Yet you never gave me even a young goat so I could celebrate with my friends. But when this son of yours who has squandered your property with prostitutes comes home, you kill the fattened calf for him!' 'My son,' the father said, 'you are always with me, and everything I have is yours. But we had to celebrate and be glad, because this brother of yours was dead and is alive again; he was lost and is found." (Luke 15:11–32 NIV)

In this story, after the son that left had squandered everything and made too many mistakes to count, he returned to his father. He was content with just being welcomed back as a servant to his family. He didn't believe he deserved anything more. However, his father's reaction was unexpected. He welcomed his son back and wanted to celebrate his return. Regardless of the son's shortcomings, his father loved him and wanted to give to him in abundance.

God doesn't want to just restore us; He wants to bless us. He loves His children and wants to shower them with more than they ask for or deserve. The heavens rejoice when a child of God returns home. God didn't just give me peace, He transformed me.

I have a beautiful, loving husband now, and we both have wonderful families that we adore. We have a church community that supports us and helps us thrive. We have a gorgeous home, good finances, great health, two adorable and sweet cats, and the list goes on. I am proud to say that none of that was my doing. Everything I have and who I have become are gifts from my Father and all honor and glory are His.

Don't settle for mediocre. The King of kings only wants what is best for his children and he has the power to bring anything to fruition. God can and will do abundantly more than you think or believe is possible. Pray with confidence knowing that you are a child of a Father who can do the impossible. You are never outside the reach of God's love.

Prayer

Heavenly Father, thank you for being full of love, mercy, and blessings. I know that my actions are not deserving of your mercy, but I am grateful that you are good to me regardless. Thank you for loving me and working all things together for my good. Amen.

Reflect

Imagine a life that is possible with God. What does it look like?

Laura Lopez-Arenas

CHAPTER 14

Our Daily Bread

When the Israelites were wandering through the wilderness, God rained down manna for them each day. He told them to gather just what they needed for that day and promised to continue to provide for them every day. In this story, we see two common themes: trust and dependency. God calls on us to trust Him and His promises and to depend on Him to fulfill our every need.

> *"Then the Lord said to Moses, 'I will rain down bread from heaven for you. The people are to go out each day and gather enough for that day. In this way I will test them and see whether they will follow my instructions. On the sixth day they are to prepare what they bring*

in, and that is to be twice as much as they gather on the other days.'" (Exodus 16:4-5 NIV)

Trust and dependency are probably two of the most difficult tasks for humans. Trust is difficult because at some point in our lives most, if not all people, have given us a reason not to trust them. We are generally taught to depend on no one and to trust only ourselves. We look at these two things as weak. This mindset is harmful and prevents us from having a thriving relationship with God.

The Bible is full of stories that prove God is trustworthy and keeps His promises. God's character does not change. He is the same yesterday, today, and tomorrow. Know that God is who He says He is, and He doesn't change. Trusting God does not mean that you always get what you want, but there is a sense of peace associated with trusting Him. Regardless of where life takes you, the Creator of the Heavens and Earth is with you—caring for you, protecting you, and providing for you.

When you learn to trust God and depend on Him for everything, you will have experience, confidence, and peace in your circumstances. Like a child who stays close to their parents, you will want and need to be close to Him. How comforting is it to know that the God who created everything walks by your side with every step you take?

On a recent road trip with my husband I had the privilege to really understand what it means to depend on God. It was our first road trip together. We flew to Phoenix, Arizona and then drove to Sedona and out to Ouray, Colorado. I think that anytime people travel, there is always a sense of anxiety about staying healthy and safe. On this trip I really found myself leaning into God. I chose to depend on Him at every moment. There was such beauty and freedom in giving everything to God.

On the plane to Phoenix I found myself cranky and complaining about a man who was sitting a few rows behind us. He was coughing loudly throughout the entire flight, and I found myself consumed with worry about getting sick. I prayed, "God please keep me healthy and don't let me get sick." As soon as I uttered the last word of my prayer, God said, "Why don't you pray for his health instead?" His words stung me because I realized that I was being selfish. My next words were a prayer for the man to stop coughing and to be healthy. Seconds later, he stopped coughing and didn't cough again for the remainder of the plane ride. Not to mention that I stayed healthy during our entire trip.

I found myself praying a lot during our vacation because I was in an unfamiliar place and God is my source of comfort and peace. When we picked up the rental car I prayed over the car, asking God to keep it functioning properly and to keep us safe. Then, a few seconds later while searching for a radio station, I stumbled upon one of my favorite Christian stations. We listened to K-Love the entire trip and enjoyed the magnificent scenery and praised God for His creations. My husband expressed concern about the truck's transmission a few times, but I was not worried because I knew God was taking care of everything.

It seemed that at every turn there was an opportunity to lean on God. While in Scottsdale we hiked Pinnacle Peak, which was a tough hike that led us uphill and downhill several times. On the way back we were really being put to the test when a hiker passed us playing music. As she drew closer we realized she was listening to worship music. I immediately took out my phone and did the same. This allowed us to focus our attention on worshipping God rather than the physical challenge we were experiencing. At every step we found ourselves trusting and depending on God, but also praising Him for His blessings.

Besides the countless blessings I have experienced, I have witnessed God working in the lives of those close to me. Many of us find God when we are at our lowest. As for my sister, she found Him during a health scare. Most likely one of the scariest moments of Jennifer's life also turned out to be the catalyst for a miraculous transformation. Whether you are a believer or not, I find it curious how amidst tragedy, grief, or challenges we all call out to God for help.

My sister's faith was a roller coaster for many years. After a series of disappointments, losses, and global tragedies, she questioned His goodness. Like so many, she wondered why God would allow these bad things to happen. Unfortunately, when Adam and Eve ate from the Tree of Knowledge of Good and Evil, darkness entered the world. Our world is full of sin and sometimes it appears that evil has triumphed, but have faith, for God has overcome the world. We can't judge God based on our current circumstances. God is always good even when the world is not.

As my sister was seeking comfort from her diagnosis she asked for a recognizable sign from God that she would be fine. After about twenty minutes of pacing up and down the street waiting for that sign from God, she resolved that He was not going to show her the red cardinal she had asked for. In her mind, just another disappointment, and another mark for all the times God had let her down. Discouraged and upset, she plopped down on the front step of the house she was selling, frustrated that God had not sent her a cardinal. Feeling down, she noticed a decrepit flowerpot—no flowers, nothing pretty to look at. But when she took a closer look she saw a tiny, beaten-up, plastic red cardinal in the bottom of the pot.

The next morning Jennifer was scheduled for testing. She arrived at the hospital early and was greeted by a beautiful nurse with gorgeous white hair whom she found to be very comforting. Immediately, my sister professed how nervous she was and shared the story about the cardinal. Upon hearing Jennifer's story, the nurse quickly grabbed her phone and showed her a picture she had taken that morning. Jennifer's eyes filled with tears when she saw a beautiful red cardinal sitting on the nurse's front lawn.

I love how God overdelivers. I am happy to say that all of Jennifer's tests came back negative but even more importantly, this became her catalyst for changing her life. The delivery of the cardinal pushed her toward her journey of putting her faith back in God. Over the next several months she began to pray more regularly, read devotionals daily, and inquire about the Bible to dive deeper into her faith, while praying that God would free her from the fears that were preventing her from living a normal life.

For over a decade Jennifer has not gotten into an elevator for fear of getting stuck. Not a huge deal for the average person except for the fact that she is a real estate agent and sometimes shows homes in high-rise apartment complexes. I am sure her clients wonder why she is out of breath and sweaty when she arrives. She started to experience back pain and made an appointment to see a chiropractor that a friend had recommended. The only problem was that the chiropractor's suite was on the fourteenth floor. With a newfound confidence in her voice, she vowed to take the elevator. I was shocked and doubtful it would happen, but on the morning of her appointment I didn't receive a call from her—I was expecting her to call me in a panic. When I hadn't heard from her by that afternoon I was sure she had not taken the elevator and was avoiding giving me the disappointing news. Later that evening I called and to my surprise she did not hesitate when she told me that she had calmly taken the elevator. It seemed as though it had never been a problem for her at all.

If you have not connected the dots yet, let me help. The only thing she was doing differently was praying and trusting in God. She was able to do it because He is now healing her wounds and giving her the strength to overcome her challenges.

"But blessed is the one who trusts in the Lord, whose confidence is in him." (Jeremiah 17:7 NIV)

It is easy to say you trust God, but the kind of belief He is talking about goes far beyond words. It is trusting with every ounce of who you are.

How do we learn to trust God? What did my sister do? She started to get to know Him. Think about all the people in your life that you truly trust. Why do you trust them like you do? You know them. You have spent time with them and you have witnessed how they behave. Getting to know God means spending time with Him in prayer and reading the Bible to understand His character. When we read the Bible we begin to know God and understand how He loves us through the countless stories about what a faithful and good Father He is. This is how we begin to trust Him.

Prayer

Lord, I have a hard time trusting. Forgive me for not always trusting you with all my heart. I am ready to get to know you. I want to experience your goodness and be able to depend on you in all situations. Show me how to depend on you and trust you. Amen.

Reflect

Do you trust God to provide you with everything you need? What current situation do you need to give to God? How can you depend on Him more?

Laura Lopez-Arenas

When We Trust God

CHAPTER 15

The "D-Word"

As a young child I feared the devil, the enemy, Satan, Lucifer, the evil one—he has many names. To be honest, I feared him well into my adulthood too. We feared his presence in our home so we never uttered his name. My mother referred to him as the "D-Word," and she still does to this day. Our fear of evil trumped our faith. Ironically, what we were doing was having quite the opposite effect. By not saying his name we empowered the devil and showed him that he could maintain a strong hold over our lives. By not telling him to get lost, we allowed him to linger and cause chaos.

When I moved to Texas I was blessed to meet many Christian women. They wore T-shirts that said things like, "Not today, Satan!" They rebuked him in Jesus's name and openly shared how the devil was interfering in their lives and trying to cause them harm. It seemed normal to them, but I found it kind of out there. As I began to read the Bible I realized why they were speaking in this way and soon understood that I would need to arm myself too.

This next statement might sound scary at first, but hear me out. As you grow spiritually and get closer to God, the devil will attack you more. Please don't let this deter you. I promise that being on Team Jesus is the better option. The devil doesn't attack you when you are walking in darkness because you are already on his team. He fights you when you are on Jesus's team.

I experienced this as I grew in my faith, but once I knew how to arm myself the devil's attacks didn't phase me anymore. I remember waking up during the night and having this terrifying feeling that evil was all around me. I began to feel anxious and afraid because as much as I tried to block it out, I couldn't. I considered waking up my husband, but I called on the name of Jesus instead. I told the devil to leave me alone in the name of Jesus. I told him I am a child of God and that he has no power over me. Instantly, my fear faded, and I returned to sleep with ease.

We are all in a battle against evil whether we realize it or not. People are not our enemies, the devil is. He creates havoc in the world and schemes to destroy us. The devil has one job and that is to separate us from God. He is cunning and resorts to all sorts of trickery to achieve his goal.

I need you to believe that the devil is real because we can't fight what we don't acknowledge. The devil is a fallen angel who decided that he wanted to be worshipped above God. Obviously, that was not an option, so God threw the devil and his minions out of heaven to dwell on earth. There are many people who do not believe in the existence of the devil, yet his name often appears in the Bible. Here is one example:

> *"Then war broke out in heaven. Michael and his angels fought against the dragon, and the dragon and his angels fought back. But he was not strong enough, and they lost their place in heaven. The great dragon was hurled down—that ancient serpent called the devil, or Satan, who leads the whole world astray. He was hurled to the earth, and his angels with him." (Revelation 12:7-9 NIV)*

You too can beat the enemy. The best thing you can do is grow your relationship with Jesus and arm yourself with God's words—don the armor of God. The devil is afraid of God because he knows he can't beat Him. So, we use the power and authority of God as our weapon against the devil. It is not by your power that you resist the devil, rather, it is through God's power. There is power in His Word and His name.

> *"The seventy-two returned with joy and said, 'Lord, even the demons submit to us in your name.' He replied, 'I saw Satan fall like lightning from heaven. I have given you authority to trample on snakes and scorpions and to overcome all the power of the enemy; nothing will harm you. However, do not rejoice that the spirits submit to you, but rejoice that your names are written in heaven.'" (Luke 10:17-20 NIV)*

Make rebuking the devil part of your prayer life. Whenever you feel like you are slipping into sin, rebuke the devil. You can simply say, "Devil, I rebuke you and your lies in the name of Jesus Christ. I am a child of God, loved, forgiven, and accepted by Him. Leave me alone."

The devil likes to prey on our weaknesses; he uses them to cause us to sin. For example, maybe you have a problem with addiction. The enemy might tell you that it is okay to go with your friends to a bar, you shouldn't have to be alone on Saturday night. While you are there, he might say, "One drink won't hurt." You have been doing so well with your sobriety but maybe you can enjoy just one. On the surface none of this seems so bad, but the next thing you know, you are drunk and back to Day One of being sober or, worse, you might fall into a full relapse.

The Bible tells us to use God's Word as our armor against the schemes of the devil. That is why memorizing Scripture is so essential. You can use God's Words to defend yourself.

> *"Put on all of God's armor so that you will be able to stand firm against all strategies of the devil." (Ephesians 6:11 NLT)*

Even Jesus used Scripture to fight the devil when He was tempted in the wilderness. Take a look.

> *"Then Jesus was led by the Spirit into the wilderness to be tempted there by the devil. For forty days and forty nights he fasted and became very hungry. During that time the devil came and said to Him, 'If you are the Son of God, tell these stones to become loaves of bread.' But Jesus told him, 'No! The Scriptures say, 'People do not live by bread alone, but by every word that comes*

from the mouth of God.' Then the devil took him to the holy city, Jerusalem, to the highest point of the Temple, and said, 'If you are the Son of God, jump off! For the Scriptures say, 'He will order his angels to protect you. And they will hold you up with their hands so you won't even hurt your foot on a stone.' Jesus responded, 'The Scriptures also say, 'You must not test the Lord your God.'" (Matthew 4:1-7 NLT)

With God by your side the enemy does not stand a chance. Reflect on your actions and words and learn your weaknesses. Weakness can come in many forms: lust, doubt, impatience, jealousy, anger, offense, judgment, and being unable to forgive. Once you know your weaknesses you will begin to understand how the devil tempts you and will be better able to guard yourself against attacks. Memorize Scripture that relates to your weaknesses, and when you feel attacked repeat the verse out loud and rebuke the devil in the name of Jesus Christ. Powerful!

I am happy to report that not too long into a Bible study with my mom, I convinced her to say the devil's name and start rebuking him in the name of Jesus. My mom is seventy-nine years old as I write this book and if she can change, you can too

Prayer

Lord, open my eyes to the schemes of the evil one. Protect me from evil so that I might not sin against you. Help me to wear your armor so that I can overcome the lies of the enemy. Thank you for giving me your power to fight his attacks. Amen.

Reflect

Are you afraid of the devil? Do you doubt his existence? What are some of your weaknesses that the enemy is preying on?

When We Trust God

CHAPTER 16

Being Obedient

Being obedient to God's will is not always easy, but it is always necessary. Often we use the word obedient when referring to children or pets. We try to train them to do what we command. It can feel restrictive to be obedient, but I promise that it could not be further from the truth when we are obedient to God's commands. God is not a dictator handing out rules and laws that are self-serving. His intention is quite the opposite. He has given us laws for our own benefit. They are more like a guide on how to live as a Christian. It is in following God and being obedient that we experience the fruits of the Spirit. Our disobedience only leads to self-destruction.

> *"When you follow the desires of your sinful nature, the results are very clear: sexual immorality, impurity, lustful pleasures, idolatry, sorcery, hostility, quarreling, jealousy, outbursts of anger, selfish ambition, dissension, division, envy, drunkenness, wild parties, and other sins like these. Let me tell you again, as I have before, that anyone living that sort of life will not inherit the Kingdom of God. But the Holy Spirit produces this kind of fruit in our lives: love, joy, peace, patience, kindness, goodness, faithfulness, gentleness, and self-control. There is no law against these things!" (Galatians 5:19-23 NLT)*

As believers, we have access to God in an intimate way for support, strength, wisdom, and guidance. Calling out to Him is like reaching out to a close friend for help. The only difference is that God's direction is always true. When He tells you to do something it is not a suggestion. Of course, we have free will and the option to follow His instruction or not, but from my experience, it is in your best interest to heed His instruction. The messes I have created in my life all stemmed from my disobedience. I allowed my desire, impatience, and pride to ruin my life. God has good plans for you, so you can simply trust in God and wait for His will to be done. Waiting for God's will require patience and discipline. Don't try to exert your will over God's. It always seems to make things worse. These are The Ten Commandments, as recorded in Exodus 20:1–18:

1. You shall have no other gods.
2. You shall not make idols.

3. You shall not misuse the name of the Lord.
4. Remember the Sabbath, keep it holy.
5. Honor your father and mother.
6. You shall not murder.
7. You shall not commit adultery.
8. You shall not steal.
9. You shall not lie.
10. You shall not covet.

My mother and I have had a strange relationship for many years. To be honest, I was a bratty teen with a huge attitude and most things about my mom annoyed me. She was a good mom, but our personalities clashed and we disagreed about everything, which resulted in a lack of a relationship with her. As I grew older, I began to appreciate her more, but my dad's illness only drove a bigger wedge between us. We argued constantly, never agreeing on the best way to care for him. Resentment and anger built up and a year after my dad passed I moved away.

My mother and I remained cordial and spoke a couple times a week. I love her because she is my mom, but we didn't have any type of relationship. The older she gets, the bigger our differences seem. I prayed that we could mend our relationship, but all my efforts seemed to fail. It didn't seem like she wanted to make any effort. I am ashamed to say it, but I kind of wrote her off. I had a really good relationship with Alex's mom and my friend Lana, who is my mother's age, so I figured I would just be grateful for them. But letting my mom go left me feeling unsettled, so I continued praying about it. That is when God told me to write a letter to my mom asking for forgiveness and telling her how I felt. It sounded like a good idea, but I put it off for weeks. Finally, I felt convicted to write it and was feeling hopeful that it would change our dynamic. My mom called me when she read it and said, "I got the letter, thank you. I am sorry too." Really? I'm not sure what I was expecting, but I had been hoping for a conversation at least. Writing the letter felt somewhat counterproductive. I was relieved to get those things off my chest, apologize, and take ownership for my failures as a daughter, but I was still angry. We were no closer to having a better relationship and this incident confirmed that nothing was going to change.

After this, there were a few incidents that proved my suspicion that my mother suffered from mental illness. Because of this, I began to have more compassion for her and wondered if maybe this was the reason she acted the way she did. Again, I began to pray, not for a better relationship, but rather for her to be healed. Then Jennifer and I had an intervention with her. We were hoping that she would speak to a therapist and maybe take some medication to help with her mental issues, but I became frustrated even further because she refused to get help.

I decided that if I couldn't have a relationship with her, I at least wanted to know that she was saved. I had tried sharing some Biblical truths and debunk myths that she believed. Each time I mentioned it she would say, "This is how I am, and I can't change." Again, my efforts left me feeling frustrated and I began to wonder if I was doing more harm than good.

Nothing seemed to work, so I continued to pray for healing. One day, I felt prompted to do a Bible study with my mom.

I was reluctant because all my previous efforts had failed, so I let it go for a few weeks. But again, I felt God nudging me to proceed so I asked my mom if she wanted to partake in a study with me. Immediately, she shot down the idea and I could feel my body getting hot with anger. I was ready to burst, but I remained silent. It was in that silence that I believe God changed her heart and she agreed to participate.

I am sure that the devil acknowledged this victory and was not happy, doing everything in his power to prevent this interaction from happening. I handpicked verses that I knew could help my mom and my sister. Jennifer gave the verses to my mom and a week later my mom still hadn't read them, which indicated her lack of enthusiasm. Finally, we did set up time to talk, but then she said something to Jennifer that offended me. I was done trying. I toiled with the comment for a few days. I was both angry and upset, but as I prayed, I realized that this was exactly what the devil wanted. He wanted me to stay stuck on offense, using it to prevent me from obeying God. Well, that angered me more than my mom's comments, and after taking a few days to calm down we had our first call. The call lasted for forty-five minutes and I was shocked at our candid conversation about God. She thanked me for my time and was eager and excited for the following week's call.

After our second call, which lasted an hour, I hung up the phone and tears filled my eyes as I praised God for His blessings. I couldn't believe the conversation my mom and I had. She was vulnerable and open about her challenges with her mental health. Together, we implemented a plan for her, and she was brave enough to rebuke the devil out loud and reaffirm her trust in God!

I would have never seen the glory of God in this situation if I had remained offended and wasn't obedient to His direction. It is often hard to follow God when He speaks to us. We want to remain immersed in our anger, resentment, pain, and frustration. It is only when we surrender to God's will and plan, that we can walk in the fullness of His glory and blessings. I am so grateful for these two conversations with my mom. I now see through Him how my mom is transforming and how we are transforming our relationship together. This is the beauty that lies in obedience to God.

I love the story of when God told Abraham to sacrifice his one and only son. This story radiates trust and obedience.

> *"Some time later, God tested Abraham's faith. 'Abraham!' God called. 'Yes,' he replied. 'Here I am. Take your son, your only son—yes, Isaac, whom you love so much—and go to the land of Moriah. Go and sacrifice him as a burnt offering on one of the mountains, which I will show you.' The next morning Abraham got up early. He saddled his donkey and took two of his servants with him, along with his son, Isaac. Then he chopped wood for a fire for a burnt offering and set out for the place God had told him about. On the third day of their journey, Abraham looked up and saw the place in the distance. 'Stay here with the donkey,' Abraham told the servants. 'The boy and I will travel a little farther. We will worship there, and then we will come right back.' So Abraham placed*

the wood for the burnt offering on Isaac's shoulders, while he himself carried the fire and the knife. As the two of them walked on together, Isaac turned to Abraham and said, 'Father?' 'Yes, my son?' Abraham replied. 'We have the fire and the wood,' the boy said, 'but where is the sheep for the burnt offering?' 'God will provide a sheep for the burnt offering, my son,' Abraham answered. And they both walked on together. When they arrived at the place where God had told him to go, Abraham built an altar and arranged the wood on it. Then he tied his son, Isaac, and laid him on the altar on top of the wood. At that moment the angel of the Lord called to him from heaven, 'Abraham! Abraham!' 'Yes,' Abraham replied. 'Here I am! Don't lay a hand on the boy!' the angel said. 'Do not hurt him in any way, for now I know that you truly fear God. You have not withheld from me even your son, your only son.' Then Abraham looked up and saw a ram caught by its horns in a thicket. So he took the ram and sacrificed it as a burnt offering in place of his son." (Genesis 22:1–9, 11–13 NLT)

When you accept Jesus as your Lord and Savior, obedience will become more natural. It will be a pleasure to be obedient because you love God and want to live a life that honors Him. Being obedient is an essential part of our walk with God. It is an act of love for God, it brings blessings and leads to spiritual growth.

∼

Prayer

Lord, thank you for giving us your commands so that we may understand how you want us to live. Help me to submit every part of my life to you, so that I may be obedient to your Word. Today and every day, I choose to follow you and your will. Amen.

Reflect

What do you find hard about following God's commands? Is it hard to follow God and live in this world?

When We Trust God

Laura Lopez-Arenas

CHAPTER 17

The Power of Intention

For many years I walked around in a fog of ignorance, distraction, and bad choices. I thought I knew more than I really did, making assumptions based on my opinion. I judged others and viewed myself as "good enough" in comparison to justify the way I was living my life. I made comments like, "I am a good person," "God, understand me." "Do I really need to follow everything He says?" This might sound familiar to you. You might even be laughing because you know that you have said similar things. I was so caught up in worldly things that I lost track of my true purpose. I was a fool who needed God's mercy, love, and guidance.

> *"Fools have no interest in understanding; they only want to air their opinions." (Proverbs 18:2 NLT)*

Living this life can feel a lot like being a child in a candy store. With wide eyes, we are captured by bright colors, sweet, enticing smells, and the anticipation of tasting all those yummy treats— indulging on anything that looks appealing and not thinking about the consequences of consuming all that sugar. That is what our lives are like. We come into this world and become tempted by all the power, pleasure, money, status, and fame. For a while we happily consume all life has to offer—everything and anything that we believe will make us happy, until the day we realize that we are anything but happy, because we know nothing about the only One who can satisfy our souls. The enemy has successfully used "life" to throw us off course.

How do we break the cycle? We find our way back to God! God is the answer to all your problems. As difficult as it is to change, you can take comfort in knowing that you will have access to God's strength, and with God everything is possible.

> *"Humanly speaking it is impossible. But not with God. With God everything is possible." (Mark 10:27 NLT)*

There is a saying that the road to hell is paved with good intentions. This means that wanting to change is not the same as actually taking the steps to change. Real, lasting change requires action and effort. You don't have to have everything figured out, but you do have to start heading in the right direction.

God will see the genuine intention in your heart and support you throughout your journey.

During my spiritual journey, I didn't know exactly know how to grow my faith and get to know Jesus, but I had faith that God would be my guide. I read a lot of books and talked to people who were further along on their spiritual journey than I was. I stumbled and didn't always listen to the advice that was given, but by the grace of God, I found my way.

Every time I made a change it started with an intention and a genuine heart. I admitted to God that I didn't have the answers, but I knew He did, and I trusted Him to help me figure things out. When our intentions are in alignment with God's will, he will make a way.

My family and friends often ask how I got to this place in my faith. This question prompted me to reflect on the past few years. Because I know how challenging it can be to find your faith, I came up with an acronym to help.

The following four actions were the catalyst for my transformation. These actions opened my heart and mind to what it really meant to be a follower of Christ. Most importantly, I had a sincere intention to grow my faith and deepen my relationship with God. Trust that He will see your intention and meet you where you are to get you to where you need to be.

Get ready to SWAP! This acronym represents a simple formula to help you exchange who you are for who Christ wants you to be. SWAP is a process that doesn't happen overnight, but with time and patience you will begin to see God working in your heart. It is important to mention that although these are separate ideas, they are interconnected. You can't just perform one; you must practice them all.

Scripture

Reading the Word of God, the Bible, or Scripture will give you guidance on how to live, love, find peace, actually be a "good person," and most importantly, know Jesus. After gathering this knowledge, it is important to apply it to your life. This is where the magic happens.

I always looked at the Bible as an antiquated document that had little relevance to my life. It was a book the priest read from at church on Sunday. I kept a Bible by my bedside, but never thought to open it. Humbly, I say yikes and admit my error.

The Bible is filled with incredible stories of hope, triumph, defeat, and failure. It is definitely better than any series you are streaming. On every page, there is wisdom and guidance that instructs us how to live a joyful, righteous life. In addition, it clearly outlines what God expects from us. Most importantly, it is how we find God on earth. The Bible is alive. It is God's living word that is timeless, never changing, and everlasting. It is one way God communicates with us and it keeps us connected to Him. Reading the Bible will change your life.

> *"In the beginning, the Word already existed. The Word was with God, and the Word was God." (John 1:1 NLT)*

> *"For the word of God will never fail." (Luke 1:37 NLT)*

Worship

Praising and worshiping God for who He is and what He has done for you is vital for change. God loves a grateful heart. He loves to be praised and worshipped for who He is and what He has already done and can do.

> "Let everything that has breath praise the Lord. Praise the Lord." (Psalms 150:6 NIV)

Praising God can come in many forms. You can listen to Christian music to worship. You can say the Our Father prayer, or you can simply thank Him for His character and what He did for us on the cross.

When we are grateful we put our soul, body, and spirit in a renewing, positive space. We focus on who is great instead of what is wrong in our lives. I praise God for big things and small things and for blessings and struggles. We praise God by making Him part of our daily lives and following His commands. Let everything you do, praise God.

> "I will praise you, Lord my God, with all my heart; I will glorify your name forever." (Psalms 86:12 NIV)

> "For you are great and do marvelous deeds; you alone are God." (Psalms 86:10 NIV)

Accept

Accepting Jesus as our Lord and Savior is the most important part of the acronym. When we accept Jesus, we are acknowledging what Jesus did for us on the cross and accepting that He is the only way to salvation. When we receive salvation, we are saved from having to pay the price of death for our sins. Salvation makes us right with God and allows us to enter into the Kingdom of Heaven as His children. Accepting Jesus means we are to turn away from sin and put our faith and trust in Jesus.

> *"For God so loved the world that he gave his only son that whoever believes in him will not perish, but have eternal life." (John 3:16 NIV)*

Prayer

Prayer is power! Period! I can't stress enough the power of prayer. Prayer opens up the telephone line and allows you to speak with Him and for Him to talk to you. Just like you keep in touch with friends and family through texts, calls, and video chats, prayer is the way to keep in touch with God. Without prayer you have no way to maintain your relationship with God. What happens when you don't call or text your friends and family members? You lose your relationship with them. Since God is the most important relationship in my life, I like to give God the best of me each day and not what is left over after a stressful day. That is why I see prayer as similar to tithing. In tithing, you give God the first ten percent of your income. I pray first thing in the morning to give God the first part of my day

Prayer is vital. Now, prayer doesn't mean that we act like bratty kids telling God what we want, when we want it, and how we are not happy with what He did give us. He doesn't grant wishes. Although, He does have the power to do anything, and I mean anything. When we come to God we come humbly, respectfully, and with a loving and grateful heart. In prayer we do four main things, which are referred to as ACTS.

1. Adoration: Praise God for who He is.
2. Confession: Ask for forgiveness.
3. Thanksgiving: Thank God for what He has done.
4. Supplication: Share your requests with Him.

> *"Always be joyful. Never stop praying. Be thankful in all circumstances, for this is God's will for you who belong to Christ Jesus." (1 Thessalonians 5:16–18 NLT)*

> *"Don't worry about anything, instead pray about everything. Tell God what you need and thank Him for all that He has done. Then, you will experience God's peace which exceeds anything we can understand. His peace will guard our heart and minds as we live in Christ Jesus." (Philippians 4:6–7 NLT)*

Use SWAP to grow your faith and develop your relationship with Him. Here, I have broken SWAP down for you to easily put into practice.

- Scripture: Read the Bible every day. Find Scripture that resonates with you. Memorize it. See how it applies to your life.
- Worship: Praise God for who He is and what He did on the cross.

- Accept: Profess that Jesus is your Lord and Savior and the only One who can offer you eternal life.
- Prayer: Connect with God every day through prayer. Talk to Him as you would your friend or father.

When we pray to God, you can pray only to God, but I believe that it is important to acknowledge each person of the Trinity for their differences. We pray to the Father when we need His extravagant love and affection that only a father can give.

> *"The Lord is like a father to his children, tender and compassionate to those who fear him." (Psalms 103:13 NLT)*

We pray to Jesus, the Son, to intercede on our behalf to bring our prayers before God. He understands what it's like to be human and has an abundance of grace, empathy, and understanding.

> *"So then, since we have a great High Priest who has entered heaven, Jesus the Son of God, let us hold firmly to what we believe. This High Priest of ours understands our weaknesses, for he faced all of the same testings we do, yet he did not sin." (Hebrews 4-14-15NLT)*

We pray to the Holy Spirit because we have an intimate relationship with Him. He goes with us through our days guiding and supporting us. He is always with us and acts as our helper. It is important that we look to Him for wisdom when we make decisions.

"May the grace of the Lord Jesus Christ, the love of God, and the fellowship of the Holy Spirit be with you all."
(2 Corinthians 13:14 NLT)

Allowing your former self to die so you can be born new in Christ is not easy, but worth it. God, with a genuine heart and intention, will give you the strength to get there. Trust in God's love and faithfulness. He is the glue that holds everything together.

Prayer

Lord, thank you for loving me so much that you sent your only son to die for my sins. Thank you for wanting a relationship with me. Thank you for being merciful and for forgiving me when I mess up. Thank you for always being trustworthy and faithful to your children. I love you. Amen.

Reflect

Are you ready to SWAP your old life for the new one that Christ offers you? Make a plan below.

_____

_____

_____

Laura Lopez-Arenas

When We Trust God

CHAPTER 18

The Power of His Love: Stories of Transformation

Before I make a purchase of any kind, I research a product—the most impactful being reading reviews. I like to hear people's opinions and real stories about how a certain product has improved their life or how they enjoy it. I am ending this book with a few stories that are testimonies of what God can do with a willing, obedient heart. These stories are encouraging and might give hope to those who have lost their way, and might just be the reason you decide to get to know God. These stories are from individuals I call my friends.

Laura Lopez-Arenas

Alex S's Story

The greatest achievement of the human spirit is to live up to one's resources and opportunities. Despite the trauma, trials, depression, and despair I have faced in my life, I've been able to not only gain control of my life, but to fulfill my purpose as I help others gain or regain control of theirs.

About four years ago I began to explore this road of self-discovery. Having just signed on to yet another prison sentence, I remember lying awake in my cell, counting the months and years until I would be free once again. Freedom is something I've absolutely taken for granted. I've committed crimes I had no business committing, spending most of my thirties inside a Texas penal institution. At that point in my life, I couldn't tell you with a straight face that I felt free in or out of prison. Galatians 5:1 says, "It is for freedom Christ has set us free. Stand firm, then, and do not let yourselves be burdened again by a yoke of slavery." Not realizing it at the time, I was a slave to my past, allowing childhood trauma to affect my way of life and my hope for a better tomorrow.

The thing about my walk with Christ is that it wasn't like you see in the movies where someone will accept Christ and everything about them suddenly changes overnight. My walk and deliverance have been longstanding and strenuous—disappointing at times, with mountainous highs and extreme lows, but my Father in heaven never once gave up on me. What's more, he certainly didn't judge me, rather, he gave me strength when I asked for it, courage when I needed it, and knowledge and understanding when I prayed for it.

I have been a Christian my entire life. I was born Catholic, but I am now old enough to choose the direction in which my faith will lead me. Looking back, I had always envisioned what a worry-free life would look like, but I never thought I would be capable of achieving it. Just one day into my second year of a four-year prison sentence I decided to attend a Wednesday church service called "God Behind Bars." It was that afternoon, as a medium custody offender with limited movement because of my behavioral issues, that I decided to once again follow Christ and accept Him as my Lord and Savior. But this time it was different. God spoke to me, reminding me of my time spent in prison. At forty-two years old, it looked like this was where I was going to spend the rest of my life unless something drastic took place. I remember it like it was yesterday, saying to God, "Father who art thou in heaven, I can no longer do this myself. I've gone as far as I can go, and I've lost my way. I want to be forgiven of my trespasses, but I also want a new life, Father God. I want a life that is worth living. Amen."

So, with tears streaming down my face, listening to Pastor Bil Cornelius speak on life change and personal growth, I became a staple at that Wednesday service. I wanted to learn everything there was to learn out about this "God Behind Bars." I learned through the prison minister, Pastor Jeff, that a church called Church Unlimited was the reason they were there. In fact, their mission statement is to take as many people to heaven as possible. Period. The next eighteen months were a whirlwind of positivity and hope. I sought anything and everything to advance my thinking, which ultimately allowed me to no longer be part of that eighty percent recidivism rate. I did it by putting Christ first in everything I did and every decision I made.

I prayed more than ever before, and I no longer felt alone. I also began to forgive those who had hurt me as a child and those whom I had hurt, whether it was my parents or an ex-girlfriend. I began to forgive myself for wasting so much time, realizing I could not change the past, but I could prepare for a better future by making good decisions in the present. I joke around quite a bit, saying that the reason I chose to follow Christ is because I now had someone to blame, LOL! Like, "Here you go God, here's my life, you mess it up. It's your fault, not mine." Having said that, never once have I second-guessed that choice, and never once have I felt that I would be better off the way I was before.

"God Behind Bars" was my life in prison and I was baptized by Pastor Jeff in the gymnasium where we attended services. Six months later I made parole and felt that eerie feeling I had once felt when I was alone, not worthy, and no longer free—even though the paper in front of me said "parole granted." That night I prayed, "Heavenly Father, please help me realize my worry that things will never be the way they were before, that I will continue to put you first in all things, and that I may in some way, SOMEHOW, live my purpose by speaking your name in the highest and bringing people to know Christ."

At the next service I told Pastor Jeff I had made parole and that I needed to put a plan in place because the devil never sleeps. He advised me to attend Church Unlimited in Stone Oak in San Antonio and told me to ask for Pastor Paul.

So, on January 17th, 2023, I was released, and a couple days later I attended Sunday service at Church Unlimited. I could not get enough of it, to the point where sometimes I'd attend both services. Then I was asked to serve and I knew I was exactly where I belonged. This wasn't just my community; this was now my church family. Now I will tell you something that was said to me. "God does not want you to be poor! He wants you to be ambitious and work hard." So I did, and the hard work paid off as I advanced in my profession. I became self-employed, the owner of Alex Plus Paint and Remodel. My father and I built a two-bedroom suite on the upper floor of my newly remodeled home for the purpose of short-term rentals through Airbnb and VRBO. Then, I took on another property's burden of debt, putting no money down, only sweat equity. I then partnered with another person to acquire a two-story townhome in Universal City, Texas. Next came a massive bumper pool, thirty-four-foot, double slide out, luxury camper that I'm turning into an urban camping-themed, campfire-by-night, riverwalk-and-Alamo-by-day. Sometimes I'm asked a question like, "How did you get that house?" or "How did you come up with that idea to make a living?" or "How are you a student at the University of Arizona as a sophomore majoring in applied behavioral science and getting ready to transfer to Houston Christian University majoring in Biblical studies?" I now own multiple businesses and currently looking for what pastor Bil called "another stream of income." If that wasn't enough, I'm also pursuing my Biblical studies degree so I may one day be a pastor and have the privilege of leading my own church.

My Father in heaven speaks of humility. He also speaks of truth. John 14:6 says, "I am the way, the truth, and the life. No one comes to the Father except through me." That being said, all of my Glory, Honor, and Praise is to my Lord and Savior, Jesus Christ, who died on the cross for our sins and then rose again. If you read my story, doubt may enter your mind because, let's be honest, a lot of it seems impossible. Philippians 4:13 says, "All things are possible, through Christ who strengthens us." I am living proof.

Lana's Story

It's a miracle that I am a believer and that my faith is as strong as it is. As a child I knew about Jesus and God, but it was not what I consider a "normal introduction," with my family going to church together and saying "grace" at mealtimes. The first mention of Jesus's name came from my mother's mother. We visited her every few months. I don't remember how old I was, but I remember she once told me, "Jesus loves you," with no description of who He was. I can still see my grandmother's tiny house—her bedroom had two rocking chairs facing each other and there was a Bible by her chair. My grandparents were not educated, and I don't remember any other books in the house, but that Bible made me realize her dedication to reading the Word of God.

I didn't believe Jesus really loved me until my late seventies. As a child, I don't remember being hugged or made to feel special and safe. I remember making sure the house was clean before my parents got home so my mom wouldn't get mad at me. When she got home from work she would begin drinking her usual whiskey on the rocks, so it didn't take long for the fights to start. I would make sure I was in bed by nine to avoid the fights and the curse words my parents exchanged each evening. On the rare occasion we enjoyed a family dinner together, I was the one called on to pray because I was the only one who attended church.

Although my parents were not good examples, the Lord arranged an example for me through a family that lived nearby. The father was a deacon in a Baptist church and his daughter became a lifelong friend. The family went to church every Sunday morning, Sunday evening, and Wednesday evening. Judy and I spent our summer days together climbing trees, roller skating along the sidewalk, playing hide-and-seek in the yard, and catching lightning bugs. Unlike my family, I never heard her parents fight or curse. I never saw alcohol in their house. Their home was calm and very different from mine.

I am thankful God put them in my life to show me an alternative way of living. The Simmons's usually invited me to attend church with them. At one of the revival invitations, during the hymn "Trust and Obey," I went to the front and said, "I believe in Jesus and want Him to come into my heart." I get chills writing these words, as it was a transformational moment in a young girl's heart. My homelife didn't change to be more like the Simmons's, but my heart and mind transformed and I was given a sense of peace.

> *"You will seek me and find me when you seek me with all your heart." (Jeremiah 29:13 NIV)*

Time passes, as it does, and my dad passed away when I was fourteen years old. I didn't understand death until he was no longer at the breakfast table every morning smoking a Camel cigarette and drinking a beer. Three years after my dad's passing my life changed. Education was important to me and from a young age I planned to go to college. My goal was to attend the University of Texas, and with all my advanced high school classes, I was on my way. While in high school, I dated Russ. I wore his senior ring around my neck, and we went to parties together and we were in love. In the fall of my senior year I received word that I had been accepted into the University of Texas. I was so excited that my dreams were coming true, but one night with Russ changed it all. I became pregnant, and when I told my mom she gave me instructions on how to abort the baby. I tried, but God had other plans. I concealed my pregnancy for the rest of my senior year in high school so I could stay in school and graduate.

As I lay in the hospital with my first daughter, my mother told me that I had just accomplished the most important thing I would ever do in my life. God allowed me to have a healthy, normal delivery, and gave me a healthy baby girl. Russ and I were secretly married, and my life went from books, homework, and exams to breastfeeding, diapers, and round-the-clock care for this beautiful addition to my life. Russ and I got an apartment together and he started college and got a job while I stayed home for five months with my perfect, precious daughter. My conversations with God at that time were non-existent, but He never left me, and He had a plan for my life.

My marriage to Russ didn't last long. While I worked at a bank I met a man named Tom who would become my second husband. Together we had two girls, a very long relationship, and we grew a connection to the church. My life has taken many zigzags and there have been periods when I didn't feel God. I know now that God has always been there, but I have not always been talking with Him, or reading His Word. You might ask, how do I know He was always with me? He is faithful and He loves me, and I feel a sense of His presence and protection. Plus, He has given me the three biggest blessing in my life, my three girls.

Through my life experiences I have discovered the importance of the church. My years spent at Bammel Road Church of Christ gave me a foundation, as well as the significance of having a church family. Here is where the Lord made Himself visible because I became a participant, not a bystander. The friendships, Bible studies, Life Group activities, involvement in the visitation team, and helping prepare for Lord's Supper Sundays all played a part in my transformation. One of the Bible study leaders made such an impact on me that I asked him if he was an angel. He later performed the funeral service for my mother when she passed, an enormous favor, as she lived four hours away and was not a member of the church. I think such a task is only accepted out of a deep love of the Lord.

During our time at Bammel Church, Tom and I and met Larry and Linda. We lived across the street from them and attended church together. Their walk with the Lord and love for family were extremely instrumental in my growth process. I witnessed firsthand "the lives of servants." They always prepared food when needed. They helped establish Impact Church in downtown Houston, and opened their home to church interns for six summers, six weeks at a time. Larry and Linda seemed tireless in their example, and they served as a comfort to my family.

While attending Bammel Church, I had difficulty becoming pregnant with my second daughter. I went to a fertility specialist and had two miscarriages. Looking back, I wonder if I had looked to science rather than to the Lord to help me resolve my fertility issues. I honestly can't remember, but I do remember the entire church praying for Tom and I and He answered our prayers. The transforming awareness of receiving answered prayers made an impact on me. Five years later we decided to expand our family and again I had fertility issues. This time not only was the church praying, but our second daughter was born. Our prayers were again answered when our third daughter came into the world.

I have developed a faith that assures me God is in control, and his timing, if it is His will, we will make the request happen.

> *"'For I know the plans I have for you,' declares the Lord, 'plans to prosper you and not to harm you, plans to give you hope and a future.'"* (Jeremiah 29:11 NIV)

I have had trust issues from an early age, but as I have made my requests known to Him, he has shown up time after time, no matter what.

Life seemed to be normal. I was teaching Spanish to seventh and eighth graders and truly loving inspiring young minds.

Since this was a provisional teaching license, Tom and I took a trip to Costa Rica to help ensure that I would succeed on the oral proficiency test. That same summer we talked about visiting my brother in Florida, but the trip to Costa Rica made me hesitant to spend more money. We decided to go to Florida anyway. Two days into our trip, while Tom and my brother Billy were golfing, Billy died of a massive heart attack. He was in his early fifties and his death had come as a shock. Looking back, I feel that God made that Florida trip happen, knowing it would be the last time I would see my brother on earth. God blessed me and our family to be able to see Billy one last time.

Five years later I was diagnosed with breast cancer. I was so scared as I carried my X-rays from one part of the medical building to another. I was by myself and didn't know what my future would be. The nurse took my X-rays, and I don't remember if I voiced my fear or if she guessed from my facial expressions. She said, "When I go through a scary situation I always repeat this over and over, which helps me calm down: 'The Lord is my shepherd, I shall not want.'" Then she hugged me. I know God was talking through her to let me know everything would be all right.

I was blessed with my treatment—I had a lumpectomy and radiation and was fine for eight years. Then I received a call from my doctor with my mammogram results. The cancer had returned; I was shocked! My second daughter went to all the appointments with me and took notes because I couldn't remember what the doctor told me. I was blessed by Darcas's faith. She kept repeating that it was going to be okay. Again, I had a lumpectomy and radiation. With God's blessing, the cancer had not spread into my body. The second surgery brought to me a boldness that allowed me to share my journey with my students. I told them I believed in Jesus and that He was going to be with me. I told them not to worry because everything was going to be okay.

Cancer has a way of causing a person to assess their life. I realized that my husband Tom and I were growing apart. He lived his life, and I lived mine. He was either working or playing golf. We tried counseling, but I can't recall praying about it. I remember sitting in my car early one morning in the school parking lot crying. I was depressed and my options were either suicide or divorce. I couldn't communicate with Tom, and I was not communicating with Jesus. I was spiraling downward and felt miserable and isolated.

When Tom and I divorced after thirty-seven years of marriage, my deep spiritual reflection began. I call it my "desert experience." Being alone for the first time in my life provided solitude, clarity, and opportunities to look deeper for answers. Everywhere I looked, the answer repeated itself, "Jesus loves me!" Those painful events and struggles gave me deep faith in my Lord. It is one thing to *know* Jesus loves me and another to *understand* that Jesus loves me.

My personal struggles have convinced me that Jesus loves me, and it is true that it provides a freedom like nothing else can. It is a warm blanket, like a baby's lovie that they cling to through dark nights. I believe God is in control of everything in the universe and there are no coincidences. I have developed a relationship with the Lord. I have found peace in my life.

I have come a long way and, through God and His love, He has blessed me with a loving family. I never experienced this kind of love as a child, but God is good and He allowed me to experience the love of a family through my daughters, sons-in-law, ten grandchildren, and five great-grandchildren. I don't take my days for granted; I focus on the present moment as much as I can. Life is fragile and I constantly tell my girls how proud I am of them and how much I love them. My daughters have brought me so much joy and I thank the Lord for every breath and every memory I am allowed to make. My journey is a wonderful, close walk with my Lord, and I am in awe. I am confident that when my earthly existence ends I will be with Jesus for eternity.

2 Corinthians 3:17–18 NIV says, "Now the Lord is the Spirit and where the Spirit of the Lord is, there is freedom. And all who with unveiled faces contemplate the Lord's glory, are being transformed into his image with and ever-increasing glory which comes from the Lord, who is in the Spirit."

Amos's Story

To the one reading this sentence, you are loved, you are special, and God wants to use you to do amazing things in this life. My name is Amos Blanche, Jr. and I was raised by my single mother alongside my three beautiful, young sisters. My father was in and out of jail when I was growing up so needless to say, life was sad. Abuse was all too familiar. Mental, physical, and sexual abuse happened to my siblings and I frequently. So this whole idea that there was a God in the sky that loved us seemed comical. I grew up searching for love, guidance, and structure in all the wrong places—gangs, drugs, sex, porn, and anger—only to always come up empty. Two DWI's, a sexual/porn addiction and facing serious jail time, I was so done. I wanted to take my life. I needed help.

It was around this time that I noticed something different about my mother. She had a glow to her I had never seen. My mother, who struggled with addiction and abuse, was happy. Why? How? I was so jealous. The constant in her life was now a church she was attending called Bay Area Fellowship. It was all she talked about. My siblings and I did not want to hear it. "If there was a God, then why us?" Typical. She kept inviting me to go to church with her. So finally, on Mother's Day, I gave in—my sisters did not. I had to see what this was about. We pulled up to this beautiful church and I was immediately accepted for who I was: tattoos, flaws, and all. Broken. It wasn't like any church I had ever been to. Once the pastor took the stage it was as if no one else was in the building. I was emotionally wrecked. This wasn't about religion; it was about knowing God loves us. He is sorry for all the hurt and pain. He longs to have a relationship with us, and that's possible through the gift of his Son, Jesus.

Now, this life change did not happen overnight, so please feel free to hear me on this. It's a daily battle. The enemy is real, and he does not want us to get to know Jesus and build a relationship with Christ. Over time, I kept attending my mother's church. I went for six weeks straight and then started serving so I could give love to others who felt alone. I invited Jesus into my heart, got baptized, and joined a Life Group. I invited those around me to join any chance I got. Looking back, life has been such a journey. I am now married, going on nine years. It's not perfect, but it's being perfected through Him. I have been blessed with two beautiful little girls, and another is on the way. Hearing my little ones pray before they lay down is such an honor. Hearing them worship in the back seat and watching them serve at our church has been such a blessing. God has used my pain to help others, to break generational bondage, and to talk about how much God longs for them to know Him. My family won't go through the nightmares of growing up like I did because I have left my previous life behind and let God in. Again, it is a daily battle, and I still have bad days like anyone else; the difference is that I know who to run to. I had test-driven the world, only to come up empty.

As I write this, I pray for anyone feeling lost, alone, suicidal, abused, unusable, or broken. You are exactly who God wants to use for purposes of his glory. He took a broken Amos Jr. and gave me hope. Again, it's not always easy, but the toughest battles are the ones worth going to war for. You are so loved, and He longs to have a relationship with you, but he won't force his way in. Let go and let God lead you. I promise you will never be the same.

Prayer

Lord, thank you for these beautiful testimonies to show me what is possible when we place our hope in you. Amen.

Laura Lopez-Arenas

Reflect

Share anything that comes up for you. What is God telling you?

When We Trust God

Afterword From the Author

A mustard seed is typically one to two millimeters in diameter. For those of you who are not so good with math, that is super-small. God tells us that if we have faith the size of a mustard seed, nothing is impossible. I hope this book has encouraged you to take a small leap of faith. Bring your little seed to God and begin to put your trust in Him. As a loving Father, He will care for that seed: watering it, pruning it, and giving it light. Through His love and mercy, He will help your faith to blossom and grow far beyond what you thought was possible. God sees your heart and efforts and will take your small act of faith and transform your life.

In Genesis 16:13, Hagar refers to the Lord as "the God who sees me." My brothers and sisters, Jesus truly sees you in your pain and suffering. Isn't that all we really want—to be seen? Well, the Creator of the Heavens and Earth sees you. He wants to know you and support you in whatever you are battling. Come as you are to God and let Him work miracles for you.

For my entire life I always had the feeling that I was meant for more. It was indescribable and I felt it in my innermost being. Decades have passed and that feeling has continued to linger, never satisfied. Now, I finally understand what those feelings were about. God was calling me to live the life He intended for me. I was made for more. I was made to serve God and bring His Kingdom to earth. I was made to do His will. I was made for a bigger purpose: to share God's Good News to others and to be a light in this dark world. You too were made for more!

Made in the USA
Coppell, TX
17 July 2025

51980094R00125